The Pastor as Worship Leader

Contents

To
my helpmeet,
Mary Elizabeth

Preface

"Liturgy" is not something that belongs to the pastor. Yet the pastor, by the very nature and content of the office, deals with people primarily through the vehicle of the Liturgy—at least on about fifty Sundays and a dozen weekdays during the year. The pastor has responsibility for the public proclamation of the Word; the pastor leads the prayers of the people; the pastor presides at the sacramental celebrations. The pastor is identified with the Liturgy by his people. Yet few pastors know how to "preside" in the graceful, knowledgeable, organized, and sensitive way which would allow the Liturgy to function as a compelling vehicle of community interaction and cohesion. Sometimes there's even an antagonistic relationship between "Pastor and Liturgy."

In recent years the demands of liturgical renewal, and the "provisional" liturgical materials produced by liturgical commissions, have caused many pastors to cry for help. They are usually not adequately prepared in the seminaries for the role of "presiding minister." How many seminaries even have *occupied* chairs of liturgics? And pastors who graduated from seminary even ten to fifteen years ago learned liturgics which are now somewhat obsolete, both in theory and practice. It's hard enough even for professional liturgiologists to keep up with the mushrooming knowledge of liturgical data and the proliferation of experimental practices. This manual is intended to help fill the void in the education of clergy for their role as worship leaders and coordinators.

A number of little "how to do it" books are coming off the press and several journals of pastoral liturgics are available (see the appendices). Also, institutes, conferences, and workshops are increasing, although they are often more concerned to disseminate information on the latest provisional liturgy than to convey a *feeling* for the presidential task and a *vision* of the kind of healthy community celebrations over which the pastor is called upon to preside. It is my hope that something of that feeling and vision will be communicated in this book.

The ideas and suggestions put forward in this book have *all* been tried and tested. I commend the Reverend C. Marcus Engdahl and the people of Gloria Dei Lutheran Church, South Bend, Indiana, for the patience they showed during the six years I was associated with them while I tried out a multitude of ideas.

I also want to thank the Reverend Ralph Van Loon, Secretary for Worship in the Division for Parish Services of the Lutheran Church in America for the advice and encouragement he gave me while writing the course on "The Pastor as Worship Leader" for the 1975 Inter-Lutheran Institutes on Worship and Music; and to the planning staff of the 1975 Institutes for extending to me the invitation to write the course. From the preparation of that course came the idea for his book. My final thanks goes to Mrs. Ruth True for typing the manuscript.

FRANK C. SENN
Fenner Memorial Lutheran Church
Louisville, Kentucky

1

Pastoral Leadership in Worship

The Role of Ritual in Christian Worship

This is a guidebook of liturgical rubrics. But at the outset it must be asserted that very little in the conduct of Christian worship can strictly be called right or wrong. Rubrical manuals in the past unfortunately encouraged a rather legalistic attitude toward doing liturgy which tended to rigidify those who were partisans of the historic Christian cult and turn off those who opposed it in the name of evangelical freedom.

The criterion we shall use is that of *appropriateness*. How appropriate is a particular liturgical act or ceremonial gesture in a given situation? That is a pastoral question. When it is taken seriously it is not easy to give away an array of liturgical recipes. Nor will it be easy for pastors and worship leaders simply to copy the various ideas suggested and advocated in this book. As a leader of worship you will have to exercise discrimination. You will also have to be aware of the true form and content of the liturgical act if you are to express that act with knowledge and sensitivity. Knowledge can be transmitted, and where it seems necessary some historical and theological background for certain liturgical acts will be provided. Unfortunately, sensitivity cannot be taught through the printed page; it comes only through actual engagement in the task.

Every liturgical act has a form. As long as we live our earthly worship will bear the features of our bodily existence. The necessity of form is especially apparent when people assemble to do something in common. Even the charismatic worship of the ancient Corinthian church was to be conducted "decently and in order." People must have some idea of what to expect if the worship event is to be edifying to them. Part of conducting worship "decently and in order" is to pay attention to what the Holy Spirit has done in history. The Spirit is not "the spirit of the age," it is the "Spirit of Jesus" who brings to our remembrance what Jesus has said and done. There is to be no new message and nothing new to celebrate until Jesus comes again, although it is still the newest thing that has happened in the history of the world. We will find plenty of new ways to celebrate Jesus' death and resurrection, probably more new ways than some of our church members would wish. But we must begin with the confessional assertion that Christian worship is anchored in the Christ-event: in his proclamation of the coming of the kingdom, in his baptism by water and the Spirit, and in his covenantal meal through which he gives himself to those who are his own.

The Christ-event determines the form and content of the liturgical act. But subsequent decisions have been made in the history of worship as well as in the history of doctrine that no responsible worship leader can ignore. There is an intrinsic relationship between *dogma* and *doxa*. "Orthodoxy" literally means "right praise," not "right doctrine." It is the worship which establishes the doctrine. Or, as the fathers of the church used to say, the *lex orandi* (the law of prayer) establishes the *lex credendi* (the law of belief).[1] If it happens the other way around, worship will become little more than a pageant acting out various dogmatic propositions. As we confess in the Athanasian Creed, "We *worship* one God in three persons and three persons in one God." Christian worship rendered *to* the Father, *in* the Son, *through* the Spirit establishes the creedal orthodoxy of the church. The praise of the Holy Trinity pervades the liturgy from beginning to end.

But there are also socio-anthropological phenomena in the determination of liturgical form and content. These phenomena draw on the evocative power of natural symbols.

Baptism is a ritual cleansing: therefore it requires water for bathing. If it symbolizes death and burial, some form of immersion in the water ought to be practiced to symbolize the drowning of the "old Adam."

The Eucharist is a meal—the Lord's Supper; therefore it requires food which is shared and eaten by the participants: the bread of companionship and the wine of festivity. These elements ought to be of sufficient quantity to establish the meal-character of the sacrament.

Ordination is the ritual setting apart of persons who will exercise a representative role on behalf of the community; therefore it ought to include such gestures of designation as the laying on of hands, investiture in the insignia of office, and concelebration with the ordaining minister as a sign of inclusion in this ministry.

Marriage is the socially-recognized binding together of two persons who will (hopefully) live the rest of their lives as one flesh; therefore it ought to be held in the presence of witnesses and be ritualized through such gestures of binding as the exchange of rings, joining the hands together (e.g. by taking hold of them with the stole during the act of blessing), and sharing the eucharistic meal.

Visitation of the sick is for the purpose of affirming to them God's will for healing and salvation; therefore it ought to utilize a medicinal sign of God's saving will such as anointing with oil, and a sign of their continued inclusion in the fellowship of the community by receiving Holy Communion.

Death and burial is the ultimate rite of passage; therefore it ought to be celebrated with reference to the primary rite of passage into life—Holy Baptism. The eucharistic meal celebrated at the funeral will also witness to the communion *(koinonia)* of all the saints.

Consecration of special places and objects set aside for cultic use requires that those cultic acts be performed in the designated place and with the designated objects. For example, the appropriate way to dedicate a building which will be used for Christian worship is to proclaim the Word and celebrate the sacraments in it.

This scheme should alert us to the importance of natural symbols and to their role in the ritual action in our worship.

It is of more than passing interest that the liturgical movement had its beginning only shortly after the industrial revolution, and that the movement has been most enthusiastically received in urban parishes. To a great extent, the liturgical movement is a reaction against the de-humanization that accompanied the industrialization, mechanization, and urbanization of large segments of our common life. Already in 1948 Susanne Langer described the fate of the modern urban worker in this way:

> All the old symbols are gone, and thousands of average lives offer no new materials to a creative imagination. This, rather than physical want, is the starvation that threatens the modern worker, the tyranny of the machine. The withdrawal of all natural means for expressing the unity of personal life is a major cause of the distraction, irreligion, and unrest that mark the proletariat of all countries.[2]

Liturgical renewal is nothing if it is not a goad to creative imagination in the use of natural symbols. But it also sees ritual as a means of establishing community identity and integrity. The mobility of modern life has cut off many people from customary societal relationships: e.g. the family, the neighborhood, the ethnic group, the church. Many live their lives as nomads and monads. Yet there is a yearning for social relationship and group identity because human beings are social creatures. People need and seek the identity which comes from association with other people who share, support, and confirm their own view of reality and who act in accordance with that worldview.

Such social groups or communities are identified by their *cultic* lifestyles. The two primary aspects of cultic life are *myth* and *ritual*. Anthropologists and historians of religion use the term "myth" as a description of the way in which a people conceptualize the reality they have experienced. It is a way of viewing reality which is often transmitted in story form: e.g. the hardships endured by the Pilgrim fathers, George Washington confessing to his axing of the cherry tree, Abe Lincoln walking several miles to return a few pennies of excess change. These stories communicate the way in which a people came into existence and the kind of virtues which are necessary to perpetuate the common life. Some myths may be more historically true than others, and some more ultimate than others. But, as Mircea Eliade points out, all myths are *absolutely* true as ways of viewing reality, especially those myths which are located *in illo tempore* (i.e. "once upon a time").[3] They are archetypal and are intended to be ritually reenacted. Ritual, then, is a pattern of behavior which acts out the communal myth, or conception of reality. Aidan Kavanagh has suggested these working definitions of myth and ritual in relation to cult.

> The functions of conceiving and enacting the values of the group *ad hoc* its particular stress-context are what I understand to be cult. The conceiving aspect I take to be myth, and the enactment aspect I take to be ritual. Both myth and ritual thus appear to me as strictly correlative and inseparable functions: their reciprocal union is what

I mean by cult. The outcome of cult, so understood, is what I understand as culture—what Margaret Mead has called ". . . the systematic body of learned behavior which is transmitted from parents to children," or what I would prefer to call the continuous and cohesive life-style by which a particular group conceives of and enacts what its values mean, thus to survive intact the stresses and threats of existence in the real order of space and time.[4]

As a pattern of corporate behavior, ritual is inevitable in any group. It helps combat group disintegration by providing a common life-style, a shared way of doing things, and an identity which comes from the outward expressions of group behavior. One is astounded at the sound ritual sense displayed by many modern secular cults with their symbols, gestures, slogans, insignia, rites, and heros. If one were to analyze such groups as extremist political organizations, fraternal lodges, street gangs, one would surely notice an intensely corporate consciousness that does not permit individuals to "do their own thing" except insofar as these "actors" are contributing in an agreed way to the totality of the event; a hierarchical orientation toward authority-persons; a feeling for concrete values expressed in body gestures, appreciation for cosmic elements and forces, knowledge of special days, seasons, and places; and simple but aggressive ritual action. No "Kyrie eleison" ever came across as aggressively as "Push 'em back, push 'em back, way back" at a typical American football game. Yet this should be exactly the model for liturgical acclamation. These phenomenological observations would suggest that, whatever else Christian liturgy is, it is a *social* event. It is something done in a consciously communal way. It is never merely subjective or individualistic. Even when it is engaged in personally, it always remains social in derivation and reference. The prayer of the private closet is still "*Our* Father." No Christian corporate worship is conducted without some kind of recognized leadership; and no Christian corporate worship is devoid of ritual acts, even if the ritual acts consist of nothing more than preaching and group singing.

In terms of the scheme we have presented, Christian liturgy is a patterned enactment of the experienced reality of the Gospel, which is the Christian myth or story. The ritual pattern which Christian liturgy takes is: *proclamation* of the story of Jesus through the Scripture readings, the preaching and the obedient celebration of the Lord's Supper; *engagement* in communal intercessory prayer and work; and *sharing* the Gospel with other members and non-members of the community when the faithful are dispersed from the assembly to "carry out" the mission of the church. Word and sacrament, prayer and mission constitute the ritual behavior which corresponds with the experienced reality of the Gospel. The story of Jesus and its ritual enactment together constitute the Christian cult. *Ceremonies* are the ways in which the ritual is dressed up. For example, it is an essential ritual act in the Christian liturgy to read the Gospel; it is a ceremonial act to carry it in procession.

If this defense of ritual action was based only on socio-anthropological principle (sound as that might be), it wouldn't carry much weight. But we will now assert that ritual action is an affirmation of divine revelation, especially of the Incarnation. Throughout the history of salvation God has dealt with his people through created means. The God of Israel became implicated in the realities of this world in pursuing his saving will. He spoke a word to Abraham, appeared in a burning bush to Moses, disclosed himself through thick clouds and lightning, carved a covenant on stone, and accepted the sacrificial response of his people. But most remarkably of all, as St. Augustine once said in a sermon, "The Lord came; and what did He? He set before us a great mystery. Jesus spat on the ground and made clay of the spittle, for the Word was made flesh."

God deals with us as we are—that is the essence of the

good news. The most basic thing we can say about ourselves is that we are creatures bound to a created existence; therefore God deals with us through created means. This is the justification for the sacramental life of the church. For this reason there is almost nothing among the great natural symbols of the world which the Judaeo-Christian tradition has not been able to assimilate; for this tradition is also populated by real people who are bound to created existence and who happen to be moved by such things. Symbols provide vital meanings in the lives of people; therefore symbolic action is inevitable. It is inevitable even without Freud and Jung. If people do not find satisfying symbolic action in one cultic system (e.g. the church), they will look for it in another (e.g. the fraternal lodges).

The Lutheran tradition at its best has been sensitive to the value of symbolic actions in the life and worship of the church —for theological as well as for anthropological reasons. Perhaps one of the most classic examples is that of the *elevation* of the host and chalice at the eucharistic consecration. The elevation had been the most conspicuous moment in the Medieval Mass. The ringing of the "sanctus bells" summoned people who, as likely as not, were tending to their own devotions to rejoin the action of the Mass at the solemn moment of the consecration. In his *Formula Missae,* Luther advocated the retention of the elevation for the sake of the weaker brethren who might be offended if it were suddenly eliminated. He hoped that sermons would teach the people what it meant so that it would not be regarded superstitiously. By the time of the *German Mass* he was ready to go more deeply into its symbolism. He taught that it was a kind of action sermon, a visible proclamation of the Real Presence of Christ in the sacrament. For a time the elevation even established the confessional identity of Lutherans. Lutherans elevated; the Reformed did not. The use or the non-use of the elevation became a profession of what each group believed about the Presence of Christ. The Lutherans held that the human nature of Christ is indivisible from the divine nature, so it shares the omnipresence of the divine nature and can be present everywhere—on the earthly altar as well as in heaven. The Reformed held that the human nature of Christ is bounded or localized in heaven and cannot be on the earthly altar, except through the Spirit. As far as Luther was concerned, to deny the objective presence of Christ in the sacrament was to deny the indivisibility of the two natures of Christ.

Symbolic actions thus serve to affirm what the church believes and confesses. This was a consistent part of Luther's teaching. There is an amusing anecdote which illustrates this in Luther's Sermons of 1537 on the Gospel of St. John.

> The following tale is told about a coarse and brutal lout. While the words "and was made man," were being sung in Church, he remained standing, neither genuflecting nor removing his hat. He showed no reverence, but just stood there like a clod. All the others dropped to their knees when the Creed was prayed and chanted devoutly. Then the devil stepped up to him and hit him so hard it made his head spin. He cursed him gruesomely and said: "May hell consume you, you boorish ass! If God had become an angel like me and the congregation sang, 'God was made an angel,' I would bend not only my knees but my whole body to the ground! . . . And you vile human creature, you stand there like a stick or a stone. . . ." Whether this story is true or not, it is nevertheless in accordance with the faith.[5]

Luther also thought it was appropriate for evangelical congregations to kneel or genuflect at the words, *Et homo factus est,* but alas, many of his followers just "stand there like a stick or a stone."

Pastoral Responsibility in Ritual Acts

If ritual serves to establish community identity by providing a pattern of behavior consistent with what the community believes, that pattern must be repeated consistently and frequently. Occasional acts do not constitute a pattern; they lack the necessary repetition. The pastor as the community's worship leader, or presiding minister, does more than anyone else to maintain the consistency of character and unity of style of the community's worship. This is as it should be. The Lutheran Confessions hold that God instituted the ordained ministry in the church. Its content is the responsible public proclamation of the Word and administration of the Sacraments.[6] Yet this has not been clear in recent discussions of the doctrine of the ministry, and it has caused many pastors to develop role confusion.

The confusion stems from shoddy discussion of the "royal priesthood" image applied to the people of God in 1 Peter 2:9. This is a typological extension of the "kingdom of priests" designation applied to Israel in Exodus 19:6. It would seem that the meaning of both texts is that God's people are bound to him by a special covenantal relationship which requires them to be a holy, indeed a priestly, people.[7] The designation of Israel as a "kingdom of priests" did not negate the role of the Levitical priesthood; nor does the designation of a "royal priesthood" negate the role of an ordained priesthood in the church. The silence of the New Testament about such "ordained priests" in the church may be explained by the fact that the church did not at first think of itself as a separate community but as that part of Israel which had come to recognize the signs of the messianic age. Christians continued to worship in Temple and Synagogue, as well as in their homes. There would be no need for a special priesthood in the church until such time as the break with Israel was irrevocable. By that time the church had come to recognize that its sacrifices constituted the fulfillment of Malachi's prophecy of the pure offering of the Gentiles in the Messianic Age (Malachi 1:10-11). Thus, Christians were instructed to "Assemble on the Lord's Day, breaking bread and celebrating the Eucharist; but first confess your sins that your sacrifice *(thusia)* may be pure. . . . For it was of this that the Lord spoke, 'Everywhere and always offer me a pure sacrifice'" *(Didache* 14).

The New Testament does not mention who presided at this "pure sacrifice," the Eucharist. There is no reference to the apostles doing it, or even to the presbyter-bishops of the Pastoral Epistles doing it. But we can be reasonably sure that someone was designated to do it. In the *Didache* the wandering charismatic prophets were allowed to preside (10:7), otherwise bishops and deacons were to be appointed who would render this *leitourgia* to the community (14). By the time we get to Ignatius of Antioch (ca. A.D. 115), only bishops could preside at the Eucharist, or presbyters whom they delegated to do this. Thus, the bishops and presbyters of the church took over quite early the function of presiding at the eucharistic celebration, just as they eventually took over the functions of the original and unique apostolic ministry in exercising pastoral care for the church.

The ontological function of the ordained ministry was already established by Ignatius: "Obey the bishop as if he were Jesus Christ" and "submit even to the presbytery as to the apostles of Jesus Christ" *(Trallians* 2). Without going into the complicated development of the ordained ministry, we would simply note that the Lutheran Confessions uphold the old tradition that the presiding minister at the Eucharist is a symbol of the Lord's presence among his people.

> For they do not represent their own persons but the person of Christ, because of the Church's call, as Christ testifies (Luke 10:16), 'He who hears you hears me.' When they offer the Word of Christ or the sacraments, they do so in Christ's place and stead.[8]

Ordination to this ministry is by God's command and it contains God's promises. The existence of the ministry in the church is evidence of the work of the Holy Spirit who has guided its development and whose charism is bestowed on the ordinand at ordination. For these reasons, the *Apology* is willing to designate ordination a sacrament.

> If ordination is interpreted in relation to the ministry of the Word, we have no objection to calling ordination a sacrament. The ministry of the Word has God's command and glorious promises. . . . The Church has the command to appoint ministers; to this we subscribe wholeheartedly, for we know that God approves this ministry and is present in it.[9]

The Lutheran Confessions assert the principle of "the priesthood of all believers," but they do not claim that the universal priesthood is to take over the functions of the ordained ministerial office. Indeed, this would result in a denial of the vocation of the laity, for which the Reformation was also concerned. Put another way, the Lutheran Confessions do not teach a doctrine of the *presbyterate* of all believers. English, unfortunately has only one word for "priest." The Greek term applied to the priestly people in 1 Peter is *hiereus*, which connotes the functions of intercession and offering sacrifice. That is the work of the people; presiding over this priestly work is a *presbyter*, an "elder" of the people. The Lutheran office of pastor corresponds most exactly with the historic office of *presbyter*.[10] He or she is called, elected, and ordained to serve the universal priesthood through the ministry of Word and Sacrament. Apart from a proper call no one can publicly exercise this representative ministry (AC XIV; Ap. XIII, 11; SA III, X, 1-3).

While the pastor, as presbyter, presides over the liturgical assembly, the liturgy does not belong to the pastor. The very word *leitourgia* suggests that it is the "public work of the people," from *laos* (people) and *ergon* (work). Nor is the pastor the only minister of Christian worship. There are traditional liturgical roles for deacons, sub-deacons, lectors, acolytes, cantors, and other assistants who help to lead the worship of the people of God. But the pastor is the *presiding minister,* and that gives him or her a great deal of control over the character and style of the service. It is important, therefore, that he or she have a sufficient understanding of the form and content of the liturgical act.

The *form* of the service is primarily that of common prayer. The liturgy is not entertainment; it is prayer from start to finish. Acts of prayer include hymns, invocation, collects, canticles, psalms, the confession of sins, the profession of faith, intercession, offering, thanksgiving, petition, meditation, and benediction.

The *content* of the service is proclamation of the Gospel which occurs in the context of prayer. Collects, psalms, and hymns surround the Scripture readings and the sermon. The eucharistic prayer is also an act of proclamation, because the content of the Christian Eucharist is the "remembrance" of Christ. Thus, the eucharistic prayer contains the narrative of the institution of the Lord's Supper. This suggests that the liturgy is primarily experiential and celebratory, not discursive or didactic. The primary task of the presiding minister is not to put across a set of concepts, but to assist the experience of the people in receiving and celebrating God's gracious gifts through Word and Sacrament. This should encourage the leader of worship to reduce extraneous explanations, commentary, or announcements. The texts and actions of the liturgy speak for themselves. If an action is meaningful enough to do in the first place, it will communicate without explanation.

The *unity* of the service depends on presidential leadership. The pastor as the worship leader should oversee the following things:

- *Preparation* of words and gestures to ensure a flowing, compelling style. Texts which are to be read need to be rehearsed before the service. It is also necessary to prepare the choreography of the ritual actions. Those gestures, movements, and actions which involve other ministers, the choir, or the congregation have to be carefully worked out.

- *Recruitment* of people capable of fulfilling various liturgical roles as assisting ministers.
- *Training* of each minister and of the worship team as a whole so that a common style and way of doing things is agreed upon and followed.
- *Guidance* in the selection of hymns, anthems, vessels, banners, cross and candles, paraments and vestments used in the celebration. Some lay people may have more aethetic sense than the pastor. He will want to cultivate these people and let them exercise their gifts. But he is still responsible for the overall unity of the service.

For several centuries before the recent liturgical renewal, the pastor did almost everything in the Service except what was sung or spoken by the choir or the congregation. Robert Hovda, writing in *Living Worship,* lamented that

> The priest usurped the deacon's role. The priest usurped the lector's role. The priest usurped (often enough) the acolyte's role. He usurped the role of presenting the gifts. He usurped part (and sometimes all) of the musicians' roles. In congregations of fair or large size, he usurped the roles of other ministers of holy communion. He usurped the role of maker of parish announcements. Except for unisonal things, he was usually the sole vocal pray-er and always the sole vocal preacher. He even usurped the role of the congregation, at least as far as any vocalization was concerned.[11]

Like so many things in the history of the church, this was more by accident than by design. Hovda admits that "Presbyters are not usurpers by nature or intent—only by habit." But this no longer needs to be the case. Perhaps there was a time when the pastor was the only well educated person in the congregation. That is no longer so. In some congregations there are a number of people who are even better educated than the pastor. In all congregations there are some members who have skills that might be needed in worship which are just as good as the pastor's, if not better. This pertains especially in music and the arts, but it is sometimes the case also in terms of public reading and planning liturgical choreography. Many pastors have hung out "help wanted" signs, and the response has been gratifying. People are only too eager to do things in the liturgy, all protestations to the contrary. The only concern here is that the pastor understand what is required of him or her in the liturgy as the presiding minister, and what may be delegated to other "assisting ministers" who may very likely be lay people.

Role Differentiation in the Liturgy

In the Liturgy of Word and Sacrament (the Service of Holy Communion or the Mass), it is the responsibility of the pastor, as the *ordained* minister of the Word, to proclaim the Word of God. This is seen most especially in the sermon, but it is also the case in other acts of proclamation in the service such as the absolution or declaration of grace in the confession of sins; the announcement of the day preceding the reading of the lessons; the eucharistic prayer; the communion blessing; and the benediction. As the *presiding* minister there are also certain presidential roles for the pastor to fulfill: i.e. the greeting or salutation; the prayer of the day; the concluding prayer which terminates the general intercessions (prayer of the church); the preparation of the gifts on the altar; initiating the greeting of peace; the distribution of the bread during the communion; and possibly the post-communion prayer.

Certain parts of the liturgy may be performed by lay assisting ministers: the reading of the lessons, including the Gospel; the voicing of petitions in the general intercessions; and the distribution of the elements during the communion. These were the acts traditionally performed by the deacon and sub-deacon.

In an evangelical service certain parts belong to the people: the singing of hymns, psalms, and canticles (for which the choir may share some responsibility); the voicing of

"Amens" and other responses to and acclamations in the various prayers of the liturgy, by means of which the people make these prayers their own; the recitation of the Creed and the Lord's Prayer; and (certainly not least) the attentive hearing of the Word and faithful reception of the Sacrament.

In the Service of the Word *(Contemporary Worship-5)*, a form of which will be included in the new Lutheran Book of Worship, the presidential role only requires the pastor to preach the sermon and give the benediction. Assisting ministers should be used in this service. They may lead the dialog, read the lessons, and offer the prayers.

As a matter of principle, the presiding minister should not do everything in a service. This includes services which have hitherto been regarded as "pastoral acts," such as marriages and funerals. Both of these occasional services have been notoriously "priest-ridden" in Protestant practice, largely because clergy have been granted civil authority to marry and to bury. But if pastors are to preside at these services, it should be as representatives of the church. The marriage and funeral services are liturgies of the church—i.e. the public activities of the people of God. There is no better way to underscore the corporateness of these worship events than to provide for congregational participation and the leadership roles of assisting ministers. The Inter-Lutheran Commission on Worship has provided for this in the proposed Services for Marriage and Burial.

While assisting ministers should always have some responsibilities, the presiding minister must consciously and visibly exercise the ministry to which he or she was ordained by proclaiming the Word in all its various forms, including the "visible word" in the sacraments and the "imparted word" in solemn blessings.

This leads to the problem of what to do if several ordained ministers are taking part in a service. Obviously, the various parts of the service can be delegated to participating clergy. At synodical or district services ordained ministers often exercise the assisting roles which would otherwise be assumed by lay persons in the parochial setting. But how are several ordained ministers to be involved in the celebration of the Eucharist? One answer is "concelebration," and that solution requires further scrutiny.

Concelebration

Concelebration has become a common practice in the Roman Catholic Church as a result of the reforms in the Mass effected by the Second Vatican Council. The reason for treating it here is that concelebration is sometimes practiced by Lutherans, especially at ordinations.

The Second Vatican Council was concerned to make the Mass or the Eucharist a community event. This meant that the numerous private masses had to be discouraged. Yet many priests felt bound by an unwritten rule to celebrate the Mass every day. In tackling the problem of multiple masses the practice of concelebration was encouraged, whereby several priests join together at a community Mass to jointly proclaim the eucharistic prayer. The usual practice is to divide the paragraphs of the prayer among the concelebrating priests and to have them recite the Words of Institution in unison. Ancient precedent is appealed to in support of this practice and it is also argued that concelebration visibly expresses the unity of the ordained priesthood.

From a sociological point of view, concelebration is the same thing as co-presiding over an assembly. In a normal assembly somebody presides, even though a number of prominent people might be sitting at the head table and even though other persons carry out various parts of the program. But it would seem to be a sociological anomaly to have a group of presidents, each of whom gives one part of the presidential address. It is no different in an assembly gathered in the name of Jesus to celebrate Holy Communion. In 1 Corinthians 12:14-21, Paul suggested that the various members of the body of Christ each have functions to perform. A workable assembly elicits the cooperation of the individual members. It is not an ideal of liturgical participation to have everybody doing everything at the same time. It is a liturgical ideal that everything be done "decently and in order" (1 Corinthians 14:40). Just as only one person should speak at a time, so as a matter of "good order" only one person should preside at a time.

Instances of concelebration in the ancient Church Orders are always qualified by a special context: i.e. the visitation of a bishop from another local church; the reception by presbyters of a local church of their newly-consecrated bishop; or the inclusion of newly-ordained presbyters in their bishop's Eucharist. In each of these cases it is more the unity of faith within and between churches that is being signified rather than the unity of the ordained ministry. In each of these cases it is likely that only one person proclaimed the eucharistic prayer—usually the minister who was being honored at the particular occasion. The other ministers stood about the altar like prominent persons at a head table. Sociological principle and ancient practice would thus discourage the way in which concelebration has come to be practiced. It is desirable that there be only one presiding minister, although other ministers may be vested and may participate in the distribution of the sacramental elements.

Finally, from an evangelical point of view the whole assembly of the faithful celebrates the Eucharist. All who participate give their assent to the eucharistic prayer by joining in the great Amen at the doxological conclusion of the prayer. In this sense, every celebration of the Eucharist is a concelebration by the assembled people of God.

Vestments

The wearing of special garments called vestments is the most noticeable way of distinguishing liturgical roles. All worship leaders, clergy, lay assistants, acolytes, and choir members, may wear cassock and surplice. The cotta, sometimes worn by acolytes and choir members is only a shorter version of the surplice. Both the cotta and the surplice are later adaptations of the alb, a full length white vestment girded at the waist with a rope-like belt called a cincture. Billowy sleeves and a larger neck-opening made the surplice easier to don than the close-fitting alb. Hence, the surplice came to be worn as a choir vestment by clerics who assembled at regular hours to recite the prayer offices. To this day it has remained associated with the Divine Office and the Occasional Services (e.g. Weddings, Funerals) while the alb has been associated with the Service of Holy Communion.

Ordained ministers wear a stole over the alb or surplice. This long narrow piece of cloth in the color of the day or season is a designation of ministerial office. It dates back to the days of Constantine when bishops and other clergy were invested with the insignia of civil magistrates. As a mark of office it should be worn by all ordained ministers when they are participating in a service as worship leaders. The presiding minister may be distinguished by wearing a chasuble over the alb at the Eucharist, or a cope over the alb or surplice at solemn celebrations of Matins and Vespers and for the Occasional Services. The chasuble is the poncho-like coat once worn by Roman gentlemen; the cope is a cloak once worn by dignitaries at ceremonial occasions during the Middle Ages. The assisting minister, i.e. the deacon in earlier times, wore a stole crossed over the right shoulder and a long coat in the proper liturgical color called a dalmatic. The dalmatic and the tunic are still worn respectively by the deacon and sub-deacon at solemn celebrations of the Eucharist.

In the past a great deal of allegorical symbolism was attached to the various vestments. Some of this was rather far-fetched; for example, the teaching that the black cassock represents sin over which is placed the white robe of righteousness. In fact, the meaning of the cassock is that it was once the normal streetwear of the clergy, just as they often wear black suits today. The symbolism of the alb or surplice representing baptismal righteousness, the stole representing the yoke of Christ, and the chasuble representing the seamless robe of Christ may or may not be edifying.

Vestments add beauty to the service and lend dignity to those who wear them. But the real meaning of vestments is that they provide a visible sign of continuity with the church of ages past. The fact that different vestments date from different periods in history only enhances this significance. Liturgical vestments indicate to worshippers that they are participating in something older and more encompassing than the immediately-present congregation. Vestments, more than anything else, are taken as a sign of catholicity. "Catholic" means "according to the whole," and it is one of the marks of the church. The church will be either catholic or sectarian, and in this day it can't afford to be sectarian. We must be willing to receive the testimony of God's people from all times and places if we are to be able to embrace all sorts and conditions of people in our fellowship. If such minor things as vestments are able to foster that kind of consciousness, they will have more than served their purpose.

2

Common Prayer
in Worship

The Loss and Recovery of the Divine Office

Worship is primarily an act of prayer. We have seen that even acts of proclamation are couched in and around acts of prayer. This means that *corporate* worship is essentially an act of *common prayer*. One of the principal reasons for the disorientation of many people from worship today is that Christians have forgotten how to pray, and the mechanism by which they were taught to pray in past centuries—the Divine Office—does not seem to be viewed as a desirable or necessary element in the communal public worship of most contemporary congregations.

This is an ecumenical liturgical problem. While the Office, or the "Liturgy of the Hours," continues to be sung in most Roman Catholic monastic communities, priests no longer have a binding obligation to recite the Breviary (the private form of the Office) and the vast majority of Roman Catholic lay people do not regularly attend any other kind of service than the Mass.

For a long time the Anglican Church emphasized the daily public praying of Morning Prayer and Evensong. It was typical in many Anglican parishes to celebrate the Eucharist at 8 A.M. and have Morning Prayer at 11 A.M. Now that the Eucharist is being restored to its primary and central place

31

in many Anglican congregations, the great majority who attend the Eucharist no longer regularly attend the Offices of
Common Prayer.

Lutherans have maintained the Office largely as an occasional preaching service. Mid-week Lenten and Advent services in Lutheran congregations often used the Office of Vespers. Some congregations also prayed Matins as the early or
principal service on Sundays when the Eucharist was not celebrated. The result of this, however, was that preaching tended to obscure the essential elements in the Office: psalmody,
the canticles, and supplicatory and intercessory prayer. The
trend more recently has been to substitute some kind of Service of the Word for Matins or Vespers in those situations
for which an occasional preaching service is more desirable
than the prayer offices. This may stop the misuse of the Office;
but it may also put an end to the use of the Office altogether
in most Lutheran congregations. The conclusion seems ines-
capable that the majority of contemporary worshiping Christians do not feel the need for regular gatherings for common
prayer.

To be fair, we should note that there are sociological fac-
tors which contribute to the abandonment of participation in
public worship other than the Sunday service and occasional
festival services. Most Christians no longer live within easy
walking distance of their parish church, which makes attendance at daily morning and evening prayer quite difficult.
Added to this are the varied working hours of members of the
congregation and the mobility of the parish families. The
variety of activities in which each member of a typical American family is involved is such that members of the family
do not see one another for long periods of time. The family
home has become a way-station. We might cringe at the
popular wisdom which holds that "the family that prays together stays together." But obviously the family that does not
stay together cannot pray together. Unless there is a re-order-
ing of priorities in most families, even family devotions are

all but impossible once the children start growing up and going their myriad teenage ways.

Nevertheless, to conclude from all this that the Divine Office is not needed or desired today would be too extreme a conclusion. The English liturgiologist, W. Jardine Grisbrooke, observes that, as far as desire for the Office is concerned, many worshipers "do not find the actual forms of these services offered to them to be satisfying—often without knowing exactly why not." [1] The recitation (sung or spoken) of psalms and canticles with a series of concluding collects does not seem to offer these worshipers the same rich liturgical experience that is available to them in the eucharistic liturgy. But this also suggests that a form of the Office that is more dramatic or action-oriented might be desirable.

Concerning the need for the Office, Grisbrooke suggests that "there are strong theological and psychological grounds for supposing that a pattern of public worship which is to all intents and purposes restricted to the eucharist—the primacy and centrality of the eucharist notwithstanding, and I would be the last person to wish to underemphasize this—is unbalanced and inadequate." [2] It is unbalanced because the Divine Office is the "liturgy of time." It preserves the theological and psychological tension between creation and redemption, between the time of "this world" and the time of "the world to come."

We do not often enough consider what it means to call the Eucharist an eschatological event. In the celebration of the Eucharist the church is manifested as the life of the world to come. This is because the Lord's Supper is the *parousia*, the presence, the appearance, the anticipation of Jesus Christ in the fullness of his paschal triumph. To participate in the Lord's Supper, the church's eucharistic meal, is to participate proleptically in the messianic feast of the kingdom of God. To abolish the liturgy of time, therefore, would empty and deprive this world of any salvatory meaning. Time would just be the intervals between celebrations of the Eucharist.

The liturgy of time exists to sanctify the day, the week, the year. It gives meaning to the natural cycles of life by filling them with the presence of Christ and his kingdom. A pattern of worship which excluded the Divine Office would be inadequate because it could not take into account the rhythms and routines of life and relate these to the work of redemption. But also for purely practical reasons, a pattern of worship which excluded the Divine Office would be inadequate because it would deprive the people of God of a rich and abundant use of the Scriptures in their prayer life. The Divine Office is almost entirely based on biblical material: psalms, canticles, and readings. We are faced with a severe enough biblical illiteracy without depriving our people of regular occasions to actually *pray* the biblical songs. And, as Grisbrooke observes,

> . . . it is not possible to supply either the balance or the adequacy except in liturgical forms carefully designed to do so: 'free' worship in the hands, and at the mercy, of a minister who as likely as not is quite incompetent to organize it profitably is no substitute.[3]

One solution to the problem of the Divine Office is to get behind the monasticizing of the Office which occurred as a result of the revolution in spirituality during the Constantinian Era. It is well known that changes occurred in the church's liturgy as a result of the official status given to the church after the ascendancy of Constantine. These changes included a "mysteriologizing" of the cult—making use of the language, ceremonies, and discipline common to the mystery religions; the development of the cult of the martyrs—the veneration of the heroes of the age of persecution, and along with that the designation of "holy places" and the erection of church buildings over these places; and the elaboration of liturgical ceremonies and architectural settings. These changes constitute more of a natural evolution than an outright revolution. The revolution which occurred was not so much in the forms and content of the liturgy, or even in the way in which the liturgy came to be performed in the magnificent basilicas; the revolution occurred in liturgical *spirituality*.

The early Church was animated by an eschatological consciousness. The Messiah had come; the eschatological age had dawned; time itself was eschatological. The *eschaton* was realized at each celebration of the Eucharist, which, as we have said, was marked by the *parousia* of Christ. The church which lived in this world neither affirmed nor denied the world. The church was in the world in order to be the agent of its salvation and transformation in Christ. The church was not a community being saved from the world; it was a community called to live for the salvation *of* the world. This was reflected in the intensely intercessory character of her liturgy.

It was inevitable that this eschatological spirituality would not be maintained in the new situation of the Constantinian Era. It is remarkable how much of it did survive. But the church moved from an eschatological consciousness to an historical consciousness. Her job was to convert the masses now seeking admission into her ranks. The principal tool used for this purpose was the liturgy itself. It had to be the liturgy because "religion" and "cult" were synonymous to the pagan masses of the fourth century. But the church could not make a missionary instrument out of the liturgy without a tremendous change occurring in liturgical spirituality. This is evident in the increase in mysteriological language and practice, which was necessary in order to convey to the new converts what Christianity was all about. But while the pagan religion declined, the pagan understanding of religion did not. The dichotomy between the sacred and the profane was deeply ingrained, and the pagan mind looked to the cult as a way of bridging the gap. As a consequence, the Christian mystery came to be interpreted as salvation *from* the world.

This revolution in spirituality left a permanent imprint on the Christian cult. Church buildings became temples, holy places in and of themselves rather than by virtue of their purpose. Consecration became an act by which "sacred" space was rescued from "profane" space. In the splendid new temples erected for its performance, the liturgy took on more of the appearance of the old public cultus of the empire. It came to be regarded as a sacred activity performed by holy men (the ordained clergy) on behalf of the worshipers, in order to save these devotees from the corruptions of the world.

Christianity, then, in the process of replacing the old religions, came to be regarded as a religion itself. The church, as a public institution, had to take on the normal social functions of a religion—what Alexander Schmemann has defined as "the sanction, defence, and justification of all those aspects of the world, society and life from which it had been cut off during the epoch of persecution." [4] The church's missionary success in being relevant to the world resulted in the loss of the freshness of the Christian Gospel with its eschatological perspective and finely balanced relationship between creation and redemption, the divine and the human, the temporal and the eternal.

There was sure to be reaction to these developments, and it came principally from the *monastic movement*. Early monasticism was both anti-sacral and anti-secular. Its anti-sacrality is manifested in the fact that it began as a lay movement, so emphatically so that Sts. Anthony and Pachomius held ordination to be incompatible with monastic profession. The anti-secularism of the monastic movement is manifested in its rejection of the church's new social status and institutionalization. Monks cut themselves off from the life of the church in order to avoid contamination by the world. In a sense, however, this was also a rejection of the mission of the church. The church's mission cannot be rejected without rejecting her worship. This, in fact, constituted the novelty of the monastery's liturgical situation: it was *cut off* from the common worship and life of the church.

At first the monasteries did not propose liturgical programs of their own. Groups of monks still took part in the eucharistic celebrations of the local churches (often to the regret of the local bishops). But eventually, inevitably, monasticism showed a distinct piety of its own. This is evident in its regard of the sacrament. Monks practiced private reservation of the sacramental elements not just for the purpose of convenience (as many Christians had done in the age of persecution), but for the purpose of *using* the sacrament as an aid to personal devotion. Here are the seeds of the later idea of receiving communion or venerating the reserved sacrament for the purpose of edification. The consequence of such a piety was that the Eucharist ceased to be regarded as the corporate act of the whole people of God by means of which the mercies of God were remembered and actualized anew in the celebration.

As the monasteries became cut off from the local churches, it was also inevitable that the process of becoming a monk would be set in competition with the process of becoming a Christian. In effect, the monastic novitiate became a substitution for the catechumenate, which was waning anyway with the increase in infant baptisms. Monastic profession, especially the practice of changing one's name when one became a monk, became a substitution for baptism. The theological implications of these monastic practices are very serious because they suggest that the monastery is replacing the church as the community of salvation, and that there are two levels of Christians: "religious" and "secular."

The most distinctive feature of monastic spirituality was its concept of prayer, involving as it did a novel use of the psalms: *recitatio continua* (continuous recitation). The idea of constant prayer was nothing new. St. Paul had exhorted the Thessalonians to "pray without ceasing." What was new in the monasteries was the concept and use of prayer. As Professor Schmemann has written, this was "the idea of prayer as the sole content of life, as a task which required separation from and renunciation of the world and all its works." [5] Early Christian prayer was not opposed to life and its occupations. Schmemann ascribes this reversal of the concept of prayer to the desire to affirm the "one thing needful" in an age which had lost its eschatological verve.

> If in the first early Christian view every undertaking could become a prayer, a ministry, a creating of and bearing witness to the Kingdom, in monasticism prayer itself now became the sole undertaking, replacing all other tasks.[6]

This shift in spirituality was sure to lead to new concepts of worship in the monasteries. These concepts were based on principles which were not merely different from, but also fundamentally incompatible with, the principles governing the public worship of the church. Monasticism is concerned with the disciplines of the ascetic life, a life lived in isolation from the world. But the relationship between creation and redemption, natural life and redeemed life, is basic to the church's liturgy. In the church's liturgy the people of God do the work of proclaiming and celebrating the mighty acts of God in this world and its history. Such a proclamation and celebration can only affirm God's intention for his creation. In the monastic life, however, the purpose of the devotional rule is to train the monk in constant prayer. Hence, the prayer offices have nothing to do with hours, days, or seasons, because such cycles of created life are unimportant to a life which is removed from this world. As Professor Schmemann writes, "In monasticism . . . time itself has no meaning at all other than as a 'time of prayer.'"[7]

We would not want to deny the positive impact of monasticism on the church. It did remind the church of the tension inherent in living in, but not of the world. The monasteries became seminaries which produced leaders of deep spirituality for the church during the Middle Ages. Their cultural contribution cannot be questioned. But, until the emergence of the friars, monasticism blunted the church's sense of mission *to* and *for* the world, fostered an individualistic approach to worship, and formed an elite group of Christians which provided the more worldly Christians with an opportunity to develop the concept of vicarious holiness. This carried with it a decline in active popular participation in worship and reinforced the notion that the liturgy is a professional activity performed by professional holy men.

The monastic concept of prayer was imported into the so-called secular churches. Many of the more important churches in Rome and other ecclesiastical centers came to be staffed by monastic clergy (an anomaly in itself) who brought with them the monastic life-style and prayer-style. The prayer offices came to be sung by groups of monks attached to the churches. The monastic ideal resulted in the monasticizing of the "secular clergy," who, by various decrees issued by Pippin and Charlemagne, were required to live *canonice,* i.e. grouped together in the service of the church to which they were attached. They were not allowed to live *vagi,* i.e. as isolated individuals. These canons were also required to recite the Divine Office. According to the Rule of St. Chrodegang of Metz (d. 766), if their work took them away from the church to which they were attached, these clerics were obligated to recite the canonical hours where they were. Hence the origins of the Breviary tradition,[8] the personal form of praying the Office. The Breviary is a useful devotional aid. A modified form of it would undoubtedly do more to link the individual Christian's prayer at home with the common prayer of the church than the countless devotional books currently provided for home use. But as useful as the Breviary is as a devotional aid, it is still far removed from the principle of common prayer.

The chief characteristic of the monastic office is the *recitatio continua* of the psalms and the *lectio continua* of the readings. This is possible in the monastic office because the monks are present at each and every prayer office. But it is an impossible principle if the majority of worshipers are not present every day at every office. Moreover, there is in the monastic office a minimum of ritual actions and ceremonial gestures. At most there is a varying of posture (e.g. standing, sitting, kneeling) to aid in devotion and to prevent lapses into inattention or slumber. But these gestures are not liturgical acts.

Lutheran and Anglican attempts at streamlining and vernacularizing the Divine Office were no real reforms at all because the principle of the monastic office was not eschewed. It was carried into the parish churches. Both Martin Luther (a former monk) and Thomas Cranmer favored the *continua* principle of psalm singing and Scripture reading[9] In the case of the Anglican *Book of Common Prayer*, even the antiphons and responsories which might have been sung as brief, simple responses by the people were suppressed. By a process natural within the Reformation churches, the Offices became chiefly occasions for reading and preaching the Word of God. This too minimized their use as common prayer.

In view of this history we might despair over ever restoring the Divine Office as "the prayer of the whole Christian people." But new possibilities present themselves in Josef Jungmann's discovery of the Office in the early church as a means of the sanctification of time,[10] and Juan Mateos' reconstruction of the shape and content of the ancient Cathedral Office, which was, *par excellence*, "the prayer of the whole Christian people." [11] Mateos has shown that the morning office conveyed a sense of rebirth and renewal, which was reflected in the content of the office: psalms of penitence (51 or 63), an Old Testament canticle paschal in spirit, a hymn of light, a New Testament canticle (the *Benedictus)* accompanied by the incense offering, the *Laudate* psalms (148-150), and the morning supplications. The evening office conveyed a sense of completion and rest expressed in the thanksgiving for the gift of light (the *lucernarium)*, Psalm 141 which accompanied the evening incense offering, the New Testament canticle (the *Magnificat)*, and the evening supplication (often in litany form). There may have been times of prayer other than morning and evening, but these were the *orationes legitimae* (as Tertullian called them): Lauds and Vespers.

William G. Storey, a Catholic layman who helped restore the Cathedral Office to current use among many groups of Christians, has pointed out that these Offices "were the affair of the whole local church, and although the clergy had special leadership roles, the daily prayers of the community were in no sense a clerical preserve. . . ." [12] They were, moreover, "both highly structured and almost totally invariable," since they were related to specific times of the day. Nor were they "conceived of primarily as instructive or edifying." While patristic custom varied, there seems to have been offices with neither Scripture lessons nor preaching.[13]

These prayer services were called Cathedral Offices because they came to be celebrated in the great cathedrals of Christian antiquity. Their theological flavor was trinitarian and christological; musically, they were sung almost entirely responsorially; stylistically, they can be characterized, writes Storey, "as reasonably brief, colorful, ceremonious odoriferous and full of movement." [14] Which is to say that the Cathedral Office was *popular*. If the Divine Office is to be restored and renewed in the parish as a means of common prayer, it is to the Cathedral style rather than the monastic to which we shall have to turn.

The Renewal of Common Prayer: Leadership in the Divine Office

Unlike the sacraments, the Divine Office is not based on dominical institution. So the pastor who is concerned to restore and renew the offices of common prayer in his parish is much more at the mercy of assumed tradition or of his own whims and fancies. If the pastor follows either of these paths, he may succeed in restoring the Office: but it is doubtful that he will succeed in renewing it. The only way to steer a course between the Scylla and Charybdis of repristination and whimsicalness is to develop a real sense of tradition. That can be done only by engaging in the kind of historical-critical work we have demonstrated in the first part of this chapter, and then to apply resolutely and radically what has been learned. For, as Grisbrooke has asserted, "it is not possible to be truly traditional without being radical, nor to be truly radical without being traditional." [15]

What we have learned is that the purpose of the Office is primarily praise and prayer, not edification or instruction. Edification and instruction occur as the Christian community engages in common praise and prayer. This is obviously a foreign concept to a tradition which has emphasized Scripture reading and preaching in the Office out of proportion. But simply telling the congregation that the purpose of morning prayer is to praise God in the morning, and that the purpose of evening prayer is to praise him at night, might commend itself.

The second thing to stress is the *public* character of the Office. It is difficult to see how any form of worship which is, or can be, celebrated publicly can be anything other than public worship. No matter how small the congregation, when it prays together it does so on behalf of the whole church. Christians who meet together for worship, and worship in accordance with the liturgy of the church, *are* the church. "Where two or three are gathered together in my name, there am I in the midst of them." It is questionable, therefore, whether there can even be a distinction between public and private prayer. Even the Christian who prays alone in his home does so in reference to the community which taught him to pray and which encloses him in its intercessions.

Historically, the private recitation of the Office has never been the *norm*. It started as a matter of convenience for those clerics who could not be present at their church during the canonical hours. The provision of a *Breviary*, a brief, private form of the Office, might still be a need which must be met;

but this use of the Office can never be a substitute for the full, communal, public celebration.

The Liturgy of Time

Because the Office is "the public and communal prayer of the people of God," it is necessary that it be celebrated at certain stated times. But these hours should not be arbitrarily chosen, just as a matter of convenience. For there is an intrinsic relationship between the nature of the Office and the time of its celebration.

Without venturing into the complexities of philosophy, we may appeal to common sense and basic theology to explicate the concept of "liturgical time." As Grisbrooke writes, "Our created nature is bound up with created time; the one simply does not exist without the other." [16] Our life is bounded by time at its beginning and at its end. In between it is regulated by cycles of time: the hour, the day, the week, and the year. If the liturgy is to have anything to do with life, it must take seriously these temporal cycles. This integration is as necessary theologically as it is psychologically. Just as it is impossible to separate created life from created time, so it is impossible to separate redeemed life from redeemed time. To try to do so would be a denial of the incarnation. As Louis Bouyer observes, "an incarnation which had not been an incarnation into our time as well as into our flesh would not have been a true incarnation at all." [17] While Christ passed beyond the limitations of time in his resurrection and ascension, he has not passed out of time as far as his redeeming work is concerned. He has promised to come again "at the end of the age." Redemption takes place in time and will only be completed at the end of time.

The Office exists for the "sanctification of time." This does not mean that we make our time holy by putting it into the context of ecclesiastical observances. Nor does it mean merely recognizing the existing holiness of our time, or of our life and work, as the theologians of secularism would suggest.

By the "sanctification of time" we mean that creation needs redemption; our fitful, partial, broken time needs to be redeemed. The Office "redeems" time by *transforming* our experience of time. In the celebration of the Office, our time, fraught as it is with absurdities and frustrations, is revealed as a time of redemption and restored as a time of communion with God. It is the *use* which makes the time "holy," its use for God. If we learn to use our time for God in the praying of the Office, we may learn to use the rest of our time to God's glory when we work and rest. This is the only sense in which the phrase "sanctification of time" can be applied to the Office; but it is not the only sense in which the term "sanctification" can be used in the Christian context.

The only way the Office can sanctify time is through the sanctification of particular times by the use of particular offices. We can only experience particulars; we extrapolate from them to universals. So, in fact, we cannot experience the Divine Office; we can only experience the particular office we happen to be using at a particular time. Thus, it is essential to understand the intrinsic relationship between the prayer offices and the times of their celebration and in this way order the shape of the liturgical day.

The Shape of the Liturgical Day

The cycles of time to which the Divine Office relates are the year, the week, and the day. The relationship of the Office to the liturgical year determines which psalms, readings and prayers are proper. In the ancient Celtic tradition, even the length of the Office varied according to fluctuations in the natural seasons of the year. The relationship of the Office to the week is determined by the Sunday (resurrection) celebration. The Sunday Office picks up eschatological themes more than the weekday offices.

Our basic concern here, however, is with the day as a unit of liturgical time. It is fundamental in determining the shape and content of the Office to ask whether the liturgical day starts in the morning or in the evening. In our culture we are used to reckoning the morning as the beginning of the day. But there are good reasons for asking whether this cultural pattern should not be disregarded as far as ordering the pattern of worship is concerned. Christian and non-Christian liturgical traditions alike reckon the day to start with the evening. We recall, for example, that this is the case in Judaism, which welcomes the Sabbath on Friday night. A phenomenon so wide-spread would suggest that certain fundamental psychological considerations lie behind it, which we should not ignore.

Alexander Schmemann writes in *For the Life of the World*, "Contrary to our secular experience of time, the liturgical day begins with Vespers, and this means, in the evening." [18] Is this symbolism artificial? Would it be just a fruitless archaic exercise to try to embody these concepts in the Office today? I think not. If the day is reckoned to start in the morning, common sense tells us that it will be reckoned to end in the evening. The consequence of this is that the evening will fall out of the liturgical pattern altogether. As Grisbrooke observes,

> In the natural rhythms, many important aspects of life commonly take place during the night—the feeding of a young child, the nursing of the sick, the not unusual occurrence of death in the small hours, quite apart from the making of love and sleep itself, the last of which is, and should liturgically be recognized as, a positive and not merely a negative thing.[19]

The positive value of rest and sleep is recognized in Psalm 4 at Compline: "I will lie down in peace, and sleep comes at once." God gives his people a time for rest during which he is "the eye and watcher over Israel." We should also remember the continuity of thought-patterns at the unconscious and subconscious level during sleep. Thoughts which should be brought to the liturgy in the morning should be implanted the evening before. The "recreative" value of the night needs to be liturgically recognized. Starting the liturgical day in the evening, at the end of normal working hours (and that is still normative in our culture, despite night shifts) ensures this recognition, and sets it in its proper context within a pattern of worship related to the natural rhythms. The fact that night is a preparation for the following day is as true theologically as it is anthropologically and psychologically. And if this sense of the importance of the night is indeed lost in our society, then it must be remembered that the Office has a formative as well as a normative role in Christian spirituality.

What are the *practical consequences* of this ordering of the liturgical day? One good argument for starting the day in the evening is that on the whole far more people are able to participate in public worship in the evening than in the morning. This is why, in the new *Missale Romanum*, evening celebrations of the Eucharist are held on the evenings before Sundays and Holy Days. It was a way of coping pastorally with the work situation in much of the Western world. It is much better that people should be able to worship at the beginning of an important Feast than to have to wait until its end.

Ideally, if the psychological force and the theological symbolism of the natural rhythms is to be embodied effectively, the evening and the morning offices need to be celebrated around the pivotal times of sunset and sunrise. In practice, especially in a northern climate, this is often impossible because the times of sunset and sunrise vary so widely over the course of a year, and the working day is not usually adjusted to them. Nevertheless, there are ways of coping with this difficulty. Grisbrooke suggests that the relevant texts can be provided with equivalent variations, so that they may be appropriate and still meaningful at the actual hour at which the office is celebrated. In any case, the principle of altering the hours of services according to the seasons of the year is not unknown in our parochial situations.

Finally, it might be asked whether the natural rhythms are not irrelevant in a modern urbanized society. For example, what about artificial illumination, especially electricity? Does this not make sunset and sunrise of no psychological significance? Few people, I think, are as technologized or as secularized as to think so. A candle is artificial illumination. Whether one lights a candle, or burns an oil lamp, or flicks on an electric switch, these necessary gestures underscore the pattern of the day. The ancient *lucernarium* of the Cathedral Office can be as meaningful in an electric-powered society as in a candle-powered one.

The Distribution of the Daily Office

The question of the shape of the liturgical day naturally leads to a consideration of the number of offices which should be provided, and of their distribution over the course of the day.

Precedent can probably be found for any conceivable arrangement. Normal Jewish practice offers a precedent for three times of prayer: morning, afternoon, and evening. Early Christian practice assumes a morning and an evening office. Some early writers such as Tertullian and Hippolytus, indicate that there were other times of prayer during the working day, but that these times were not obligatory, and may not even have been communal. The developed Cathedral Office provides for morning and evening prayer, plus an occasional Vigil on the eves of certain festivals. The developed monastic Office in the West comprises six, seven, or eight offices; the later Byzantine monastic style had as many as eleven or twelve offices at certain times of the year. Mateos points out that the Chaldean Rite provides for a daily cycle of four or five offices. W. S. Porter demonstrates the example of a monastic rite in Spain comprising no less than twenty-four hours of prayer.[20]

It would seem, then, that the provision of a daily morning and evening office is the minimum which makes sense liturgically, and probably also the maximum which makes sense practically. The Vigil Office has considerable theological and psychological value in marking out certain important days; but it doesn't have much practical pastoral value. We would be fortunate if we could get our people to participate in a proper vigil at least on the eves of Easter, Pentecost and Christmas. With student groups and retreats, however, it should be possible to hold a vigil on the eve of the Sunday celebration. A structure for such a vigil might be the following:

Antiphon
Office Hymn (during which a large candle—i.e. the paschal candle—is placed in its stand, and altar lights are lighted).
Thanksgiving for the gift of light.

This is followed by 4 sets of 3 biblical readings, each reading selected because it relates to the Sunday theme; silence is kept at the end of each reading, after which the presiding minister says, "Let us pray"; then he or the reader offers a short prayer which arises from the text of the reading. After each three readings, a psalm or canticle is sung. Thus, the structure might be:

Psalm 141 (with incensation)
3 lessons
Psalm w/collect
3 Lessons
Psalm w/collect
3 Lessons
Psalm w/collect
3 Lessons
Canticle (e.g. *Te Deum*)

The *relationship of the Office to the Eucharist* calls for consideration. The Eucharist, after all, is normally preceded by a form of the Office—the liturgy of the Word. It might well be asked whether the daily Offices should not take the form of morning and evening services with the Eucharist added to one or both of them, in accordance with devotional desire or practical necessity. This might eliminate the problem of repetition which sometimes occurs when Matins or Vespers is held preceding or following the Eucharist, and elements common to both (i.e. psalmody and readings) are duplicated. But there are disadvantages to this scheme: *First,* there is the danger of the Eucharist coming to be regarded as an appendage to the office (as it sometimes is in Lutheran practice). Or, alternately, the office could come to be treated as merely preliminary to the Eucharist (a trap Roman Catholics and Anglicans especially might fall into). *Second,* the intimate link between the Liturgy of the Word (the ancient Synagogue office) and the Liturgy of the Eucharistic Meal ought not to be obscured. The Word is really not the predominant aspect of the prayer offices; and a full concept of commemoration or *anamnesis* necessitates that at the eucharistic liturgy the proclamation of the mighty acts of God in salvation history, through the readings and the sermon not be blunted. *Third,* if the Eucharist were combined with the Office, precisely this might happen: that the Office is reduced to little more than a liturgy of the Word. Thus it would cease to be a "liturgy of time." *Finally,* such an arrangement would further complicate the task of compiling a logical and meaningful scheme of scripture readings appropriate to the Office.

We turn now to the issue of *the lesser hours.* It might be tempting simply to abandon them altogether, but this approach is perhaps too purist. For practical reasons, the lesser hours should not be included in the basic round of offices. Nevertheless, there are situations for which such offices could be useful, especially in retreat situations. As a minimum, therefore, a noon or midday office should be provided by combining Terce, Sext, and None. *The Worship Supplement* prepared by the Commission on Worship of the Lutheran Church-Missouri Synod has provided such a Noonday Office.

Like the interval hours (the day-time offices), the offices
of Prime and Compline originated as private devotions. It is
not easy to envision a pastoral situation today in which Prime
would be either required or desired. Its position would be
absorbed by a communal celebration of Lauds, or Morning
Prayer. The same cannot be said of Compline. Probably the
reason this office has enjoyed a real popularity in the West
is because its contents are appropriately related to the time
of the day at which it is recited—bedtime. In other words,
although it is a monastic office in origin, its spirit is that of
the cathedral office. Compline can be meaningfully used as
prayer at the close of the day, unless a Vigil is to be held
(in which case Compline would be suppressed).

The *Worship Supplement* has provided a form of Compline
which is faithful to the traditional structure of this office. A
form of Compline will also be provided in the new Lutheran
Book of Worship. One of the most noteworthy features of
this office is the mutual act of confession between minister
and people. This *confiteor* ("I confess") became the earliest
form of confession of sins before the beginning of the Mass,
and its restoration as a preparatory office for the eucharistic
liturgy would be most appropriate. It should also be noted
that if Vespers is celebrated on the same evening as Compline, the *Magnificat* is the canticle at Vespers and the *Nunc
dimittis* is always the canticle at Compline.

This leaves the shape and content of the two principal daily
offices to be determined: *Lauds* and *Vespers*. Perhaps one of
the most significant efforts at reforming and renewing the
Cathedral Office in recent years has taken place at the University of Notre Dame under the leadership of Dr. William
G. Storey. The Notre Dame Office Book, *Morning Praise and
Evensong*, which provides fully sung offices for every day of
the week, draws on the work of Juan Mateos, and much of its
content reveals the inspiration of the Byzantine Daily Office.
We have not dealt with the Byzantine Office. By the time of
the high middle ages it too was strongly determined by mon-

astic usages; but it has preserved far more elements of the
Cathedral rite than has its Roman counterpart. This is evident,
for example, in the retention of the *lucernarium* in Vespers
and in the singing of litanies in all the offices. It's not a kind
of office which lends itself to private recitation. Indeed, the
corporate liturgical concepts of the Eastern church do not lend
themselves very easily to purely individual devotion. This corporate consciousness has helped to keep alive the choral recitation of the office in the Eastern churches. The Notre Dame
Office takes the following shape:[21]

Morning Praise	**Evensong**

I. *Invitatory*

a. Versicle and Response: doxological in character: derived from Byzantine Offices.	a. Versicle and Response: "Jesus Christ is the light of the world. R/A light no darkness can extinguish."
b. Morning Hymn (sometimes based on Ps. 95, the Venite Exultemus)	b. Evening hymn (expressing a light theme)
c. Salutation and Collect	c. Thanksgiving for Light

II. *Psalmody*

a. Morning Psalm (penitential or supplicatory in nature)	a. Psalm 141 (invariable)
b. Old Testament Canticle	b. Evening Psalm
c. Praise Psalm (pss. 148-150)	c. New Testament Canticle

III. *Readings*

(Usually one reading, followed by a period of silent meditation
and/or a homily)

IV. *The Gospel Canticle*

The Song of Zechariah (Benedictus)	The Song of Mary (Magnificat) on Sundays and Festivals; The Song of Simeon (Nunc dimittis) on weekdays.

V. *The Intercessions*

Morning supplication in the form of Preces, or Suffrages (responsive type of prayer): concluding collect.	Evening intercessions in litany form inspired by the Byzantine style; concluding collect.

VI. *The Lord's Prayer*

VII. *The Blessing*
Simple Form   Solemn Form

The use of this Office in various university, parochial and religious communities has proven the "popular" character of the cathedral rite over the monastic rite. This is due in large part to the greater feeling of involvement created, especially in Evensong, by the candle-lighting ceremony, the incensation, and the sung litanies. The use of psalm collects also aids in actually praying the Psalms.

The Inter-Lutheran Commission on Worship has cast a favorable eye on this Office. At least the *lucernarium* will be restored to Vespers in the new Lutheran Office. The drafting sub-committee took so seriously the principle of "Involvement-through-action" which is characteristic of the Cathedral Office that it looked for some ritual action to incorporate into Matins which would be comparable to the *lucernarium* in Vespers. The subcommittee found such a ritual in the Little Office of the Resurrection, which was a popular devotion during the late Middle Ages. Styled "the Paschal Blessing," it will conclude Morning Prayer on Sundays except during Advent and Lent. This Little Office is conducted at the baptismal font and includes the reading of the resurrection Gospel, the singing of the *Te Deum*, and a concluding blessing. The sprinkling of the people with water from the font as a reminder of their Baptism would appropriately follow. Or, people might be encouraged to dip their hand in the font as they leave the church and trace on themselves the cross of Christ with which they were sealed for eschatological salvation at their Baptism. Such ceremonies will make the Office once again a liturgical act, and not simply an edifying devotion.

The Celebration of Morning Praise and Evensong

Matins and Vespers in the Lutheran church have been celebrated as public offices, although often with more solemnity than they require. The offices are flexible liturgies capable of being adapted to varied situations. In my present parish Matins is prayed in a fellowship hall around a work table. Except during Lent, Vespers is prayed in a chapel. Vestments are not used. However, our concern here is with a more solemn setting.

The Office does not require the use of the altar. The presiding minister may remain at his chair throughout most of the Office. Nor does he need to take most of the parts. Presidential roles consist primarily of offering collects at the end of the psalms and supplications, censing the altar during the Gospel canticle if and when this is done, and giving the benediction. Traditional diaconal roles at Vespers include carrying in the Vespers—candle (which might be the paschal candle), offering the Thanksgiving for light, censing the ministers and people during the singing or saying of Psalm 141, and leading the petitions of the supplicatory prayer. The cantor leads the singing of the psalms and canticles and a lector reads the lesson. If vestments are used, all the ministers may wear albs, or cassocks and surplices, the presiding minister also wearing a stole.

The *lucernarium* at Vespers requires the use of a large candle which is carried in procession to its stand. The focus of the Office is neither the altar nor the ambo, but the praying community. So the candle might be placed in the "midst" of the people. It is effective at Vespers to light other candles during the singing of the evening hymn. This might be done by acolytes.

The *incensation* at Vespers takes place during Psalm 141 ("Let my prayer rise before you as incense:/ the lifting up of my hands as the evening sacrifice"); it may also occur during the *Magnificat*. The most traditional and solemn manner of incensing is to swing a thurible (censer) in the direction of objects used in worship (e.g. the paschal candle, the altar) and the people. In less solemn celebrations the incense might simply be burned in a bowl on the altar or on a small table placed next to the paschal candle.

If incense is introduced to a congregation, its meanings will most likely have to be elaborated. Most basically, "incense owns a deity nigh" (as the familiar Epiphany carol, "We Three Kings," puts it); it symbolizes the presence of God among his people. This is the meaning associated with incense at the Gospel canticle. Incense is also a form of visible prayer (Psalm 141), a symbol of the prayers of the faithful rising to God (Rev. 5:8; 8:3-4). Related to this is its purificatory significance, not only hygenically, but as a visible sign of absolution (Num. 16:46ff.). These latter two meanings of incense are associated with its use during the Vespers-psalm.

It needs to be candidly admitted that few things turn off many Protestants as much as incense does. Some of the antipathy toward incense may be anti-(Roman) Catholic sentiment. But the fact that some modern Roman Catholics find incense "outdated" or "irrelevant" suggests that there are also strong strains of rationalism and spiritualism present in modern Western society, and something as obviously primitive, earthy and mystical as incense brings these strains to a head. Rationalism and spiritualism present serious pastoral problems, because they render very difficult the apprehension of sacramental reality.

Something should also be said about two elements which have come almost to dominate the Lutheran Office: the use of hymns and the sermon. In both Matins and Vespers, there is provision for the Office Hymn. In traditional usage, this is a morning or an evening hymn. Both the SBH and TLH have provided some examples of classical office hymns.

Morning:	**Evening:**
SBH	*SBH*
204 (Christe sanctorum)	219 (Strength and Stay)
206 (Splendor paternae)	220 (Pros hilaron)
133 (O lux beata Trinitas)	
TLH	*TLH*
550 (Splendor paternae)	555
564 (O lux beata Trinitas)	101 (Pros hilaron)

Of course, any hymn in the morning or evening sections of the hymnal would be appropriate. On major festivals, such as Christmas and Easter and Pentecost, it would be appropriate to sing a hymn for that feast-day. Otherwise, to maintain the character of the Office as a liturgy of time it is best to use hymns related to the hour of the day at which the office is held.

The Offices do not provide for processional and recessional hymns. On normal days, even when a choir is present leading the singing, it is appropriate for the choir and ministers to go directly to their places without singing. Processional and recessional hymns to accompany the entrance of the choir and clergy might be reserved for major festivals, since processions are one way to dress up a festival.

The Divine Office is a service of praise and prayer; it is not a preaching office. The provision of hymns, psalms, lessons, responsories, canticles and prayers are adequate without an address. If there is preaching at the Office, it should be confined to a brief homily on the reading or a narrative on the life of a saint if it is a saint's day. (For material on the saints see Butler's *Lives of the Saints,* revised by Herbert Thurston and Donald Attwater.) It would also be appropriate to read a brief selection from the writings of the Fathers. It is inappropriate to deliver a full sermon at the Office. If preaching is desired it would be better to use the Service of the Word (CW-5). The place of the homily in the proposed Lutheran Office (CW-9: *Daily Prayer of the Church)* is at the end of the Office.

The Use of the Office in the Parish

In Lutheran parishes, Vespers has been used as a mid-week service during Lent and less frequently during Advent. Matins has sometimes been used as an early service on Sunday mornings. Some parishes arrange morning and evening prayer for their staffs. So our people have some acquaintance with the

Divine Office, but not enough acquaintance to be aware of its character as the liturgy of time.

The only way to increase the frequency of usage is to increase the frequency of usage. The Divine Office is the prayer of the church. Instead of providing "pick-up devotions" for meetings of the church council, parish auxiliaries, and study groups, the pastor should provide the offices of morning and evening prayer. Even if there is no time for a fully sung office, it is possible to pray morning and evening prayer in simpler forms. A brief form of Matins includes the opening versicles, a psalm, a reading, the Benedictus, a morning prayer, the Lord's Prayer, and the blessing. A brief form of Vespers includes the opening versicles, the light hymn *(Phos hilaron)*, the thanksgiving for light, Psalm 141, a reading, the Magnificat, the Lord's Prayer, and the blessing. In these simplified forms, Matins and Vespers can also be prayed in the family home.

We have devoted this much space to the Office because the restoration of daily common prayer is as essential for renewing the life of the church as the restoration of the Eucharist to the center of the church's life. It is through the use of the Office that the church has learned to pray in each generation throughout its history. Moreover, this prayer which is the prayer of the church is also the prayer of Christ. This was the fundamental insight of the fathers in their commentaries on the Psalms. They saw Christ as the object and content of the psalms. To pray the psalms is to surrender oneself to God's work of creation and redemption which is fulfilled in Christ.

The prayer of Christ is also the work of Christ; so the prayer of the church is also the work of the church through the Spirit of Christ who groans within and causes her both to will and to do. When we pray for someone we intend thereby to accomplish something for that person. When we praise God, he is glorified in his creation. This is the true priestly ministry of the church: to intercede on behalf of the world because the world cannot pray for itself, and to offer the world to God in a sacrifice of love and praise. When the church understands this to be her true work, she will gather for prayer on some regular basis. She will gather when her needs and her faith draw her together, and even when they don't. Only through *disciplined* gatherings for common prayer can the church fulfill the work she has set out for herself when she says, "Let us pray."

3

Initiation into Worship

Leadership in Christian Initiation

There is no doubt that it is the scandal of Christians rather
than the scandal of the Gospel which has turned many people away from the church in recent years. The response of
the pagans to the life-style of the early Christians has not
often been elicited in subsequent centuries: "See how these
Christians love one another." Our concern in the chapter on
"Common Prayer as Worship" was the formation of a Christian community whose corporate life is consonant with the
call of the Gospel and the demands of the kingdom. Renewal
in Christian initiation is impossible unless there actually
exists a community which is capable of the conversion and
subsequent nurturing of those who are newly born in Christ.
For Baptism amounts to a kind of charter of the church's
existence. Each celebration of Holy Baptism not only incorpo-
rates new members into the church, but it also reminds the
church of who it corporately is and what it is expected to be.
The Liturgy of Holy Baptism must be constructed in such a
way that it can ritualize this reality. We shall first see what
is happening in the baptismal act, and what this implies for
the baptismal rite and life. Then we shall see how the new
rite prepared by the Inter-Lutheran Commission on Worship
handles the experience of Christian initiation. Finally, we
shall suggest ways of performing this rite effectively.

Baptismal Theology and Its Implications
for Worship Practices

Baptism is preeminently the work of God. He acts in this sacrament to enlarge his family and to save them through their identification with the crucified and risen Lord Jesus Christ. Our adoption as new sons and daughters of God is possible because when we are assigned to the lordship of Jesus we are also given the gift of forgiveness which he won for us through his atoning death on the cross. To be assigned to the person of Jesus is also to be assigned to his history. This is the central theme of St. Paul's baptismal theology, and it is also the central baptismal teaching of the Lutheran Catechisms. Neither St. Paul nor Luther dealt with the philosophic problem of the time-interval posed in the assertion that the death of Christ and our death in the waters of Baptism are *one* event. But both are concerned about the effects of this identification: that "our old self was crucified with him so that the sinful body might be destroyed, and we might no longer be enslaved to sin" (Rom. 6:6). Baptism "effects forgiveness of sins, delivers from death and the devil, and grants eternal salvation to all who believe, as the Word and promise of God declare" *(Small Catechism* IV, 6).[1]

In preaching and teaching, the pastor must emphasize what God is doing in Holy Baptism and what the results are for Christian life. This can be done only by asserting our identification with the history of Jesus' death and resurrection, our participation in his passover from death to life. Edmund Schlink laments that "the separation of the understanding of Baptism from the history of Jesus Christ is more widespread than the history of the dogma of Baptism would lead us to suspect. In many churches the preaching about Baptism not infrequently confines itself to very general statements about the promise of grace which God imparts through Baptism."[2] We would add that this happens because Baptism is all too frequently separated from its paschal context: the Easter Vigil.

To be baptized in the name of Jesus is to be baptized by the Spirit of Jesus. This was the common conviction of the early church: "You were washed, you were sanctified, you were justified in the name of the Lord Jesus Christ and in the Spirit of our God" (1 Cor. 6:11). The gift of the Holy Spirit given in Baptism is shared by all the members of the church, for only those who receive the Spirit of Jesus can say "Jesus is Lord." The fellowship of the church is the fellowship of the Spirit who "calls, gathers, enlightens and sanctifies the whole Christian church on earth."

This has certain implications for liturgical practice. It suggests that no one should be baptized apart from the church (i.e. the assembly of God's people) except in cases of dire emergency. Baptism may be intensely personal, but it is not individualistic. It concerns the whole church, which is the fellowship of the Holy Spirit. The corporate nature of Baptism can be underscored by giving the congregation a more active role in the celebration of the Liturgy of Holy Baptism. It can also be underscored if Baptism is celebrated in the context of the eucharistic liturgy since the body of Christ in this world is manifested and realized in the Lord's Supper. Baptism as the church's rite of initiation is incorporation into the body of Christ. Reception of Baptism should therefore lead to reception of Holy Communion.

The resurrection from the dead and the outpouring of the Holy Spirit on "the last and great day" (Pentecost) are eschatological events. To pass over from death to life in the Spirit of Jesus is an eschatological experience. Therefore, Baptism is an eschatological act. To be assigned to the person of Jesus in his death and resurrection by the work of his Spirit is to be assigned to his future. "For if we have been united with him in a death like his, we shall certainly be united with him in a resurrection like his" (Rom. 6:5). The whole life of the church is animated by this hope of future fulfillment. Thus, the new community which is established and enlarged through Holy Baptism is an eschatological community. This again has certain implications for our baptismal practice.

The Liturgy of Holy Baptism must connect each person with God's promise in Christ and with the community which inheres in him. This eschatological view of Baptism thus provides a theological defense for the baptism of infants and young children. It is noteworthy that the rationale for infant baptism in the Lutheran Confessions is not based on the argument of original sin, but on the command and promise of God.

> The *promise* of salvation pertains also to little children, but it does not pertain to those outside of Christ's Church, where there are neither Word nor Sacraments, because the Kingdom of Christ exists only with the Word and Sacraments. Therefore it is necessary to baptize little children, that the promise of salvation may be applied to them, according to Christ's command in Matthew 28:19, "Baptize all nations." Just as here salvation is offered to all, so Baptism is offered to all, to men, women, children, and infants. (Apology IX, 52).[3]

All people are baptized in the *hope* of the fulfillment of the promise of salvation. This hope is based on God's Word, which has proven itself trustworthy in the past, especially in the resurrection of Jesus. In this we have the pledge of our own resurrection and of the transformation of all things in Christ. To base Baptism on original sin often leads to a quasi-magical, *opus operatum* view of Baptism which undercuts its corporate dimension. Baptism then becomes a semi-private clinical act performed in order to remove the birth defect of original sin. The eschatological view of Baptism underscores the corporate dimension of this sacrament because the entire community is the heir of God's promises. It is natural for children born into the community of promise to be connected with that promise by being personally sealed as God's own.[4] On the other hand, it would appear to be unnatural to *indiscriminately* baptize the children of parents who are not active members of the community of promise. If children of non-church members are to be baptized, the role of sponsorship will have to be once again taken seriously. Favorite aunts and uncles who are not active church members will not do. The sponsors must be committed members of the community of promise, which suggests that members of the local community in which the Baptism is celebrated would make the most appropriate sponsors. Ultimately, the whole congregation is the sponsor of Baptism. The role of sponsorship must be taken no less seriously with adult candidates. They too need to be guided into the life of the community.

If Baptism is an eschatological event, it signifies a demarcation between the new and the old in the baptized person's life. In a comparative study of initiation, Mircea Eliade has suggested that initiation is "equivalent to a basic change in existential condition; the novice emerges from his ordeal with a totally different being from that which he possessed before his initiation; he has become *another*." [5] This is exactly the claim St. Paul makes: "We were buried therefore with him by baptism into death, so that as Christ was raised from the dead by the glory of the Father, we too might walk in newness of life" (Rom. 6:4).

Baptism is a once-for-all event; but it initiates an ongoing dynamic in Christian life. One emerges from Baptism with a new status, as a new person, a "new Adam." Christian life after Baptism must reflect this fundamental change in existential condition. Luther commented on this continuing significance of Baptism in Christian life in his discussion of the significance of the baptismal water: "It signifies that the old Adam in us, together with all sins and evil lusts, should be drowned by daily sorrow and be put to death, and that the new man should come forth daily and rise up, cleansed and righteous, to live forever in God's presence" (*Small Catechism* IV, 12). [6]

Luther is also credited with having said that the old Adam is a mighty good swimmer who doesn't drown easily in the waters of Baptism. It's another way of saying that even though we are called to the life of holiness in Baptism, we remain sinners who live in tension between the old life and the new. Baptism forgives sin, it does not remove it. For this reason formal opportunity must be provided for "daily sorrow and repentance" to take place. The Office of the Keys affords this opportunity. Confession and absolution is always a reminder of the primal gift of forgiveness bestowed in Holy Baptism. Even though we sin and must return to God, we still have access to this gift. The private form of confession is preferable to the public form because it allows the penitent to be specific and to hear the word of grace applied specifically to him. In the concrete word addressed personally to the penitent, there is a real assurance of forgiveness. Indeed, the form of private confession in Luther's Catechism includes the question, "Do you believe that the forgiveness I declare is the forgiveness of God?" If the penitent cannot answer, "Yes, I do," there is no point in the pastor proceeding with the absolution. If the penitent can answer affirmatively, then an assurance can be conveyed which cannot always be assumed to be conveyed in the Order for Public Confession. The Office of the Keys is one of the great treasures of the church, a means of grace, and pastors should provide opportunity for their members to make use of it. A form modeled on Luther's in the Catechism is provided in the *Worship Supplement* prepared by the Commission on Worship of the Lutheran Church—Missouri Synod (1969).

Because Baptism initiates an ongoing dynamic in Christian life, it has been viewed as ordination to service in God's kingdom. The command to baptize was given concomitantly with the command to proclaim the Gospel to all nations. Baptism and mission are thus joined together in the dominical institution. Edmund Schlink observes, "It is important for understanding the ecclesiological significance of Baptism that the

divine act of being received into the church is not separated
from the divine command under which the church stands
together with each of her members." [7] Baptism is possible
only because the church is engaged in mission and is bringing the good news to people with an invitation to join the
community of promise and share in her life and mission.
Those who are baptized receive from the Holy Spirit the
power of faith which enables them to be engaged in the mission of the church. The invocation of the Holy Spirit and the
anointing can be seen as the specific ordination to service in
God's kingdom. The presentation of the lighted candle can
also be seen as a reminder that the baptized person is to be
engaged in prayer and works of ministry.

This is a heavy load to hang on the Sacrament of Baptism.
The only way all this can be accomplished is through the
restoration of a viable pre- or post-baptismal catechumenate
of sufficient intensity to form the individual into the life-style
of the eschatological community. The Liturgy of Holy Baptism will not work in the ways we have described it unless
there is an educational machinery capable of supporting it.
We cannot be reminded too often of Tertullian's saying that
"Christians are made, not born."

New Elements in the Liturgy of Holy Baptism

Having isolated some important aspects of baptismal meaning and their implications for worship, we can now see what
the proposed ILCW Liturgy of Holy Baptism attempts to do in
renewing our practice of Christian initiation.[8] There is no
attempt here to harmonize all of the foregoing with elements
in the new rite. That would be eisegesis rather than exegesis.
Rather, the reader may draw his own conclusions about how
adequately the new rite has met the implications for worship
we have suggested above.

Theology maintains that baptism is the premier event in
Christian life. Yet our practice of Baptism would not convey
such an impression. Eugene Brand reminds us that "Larger

parishes have scheduled Baptisms at times other than the community's regular worship, rather effectively obscuring the communal aspect of the sacrament. Where baptisms do take place within the Sunday service, they are often gotten through as quickly as possible, leaving the impression of 'please forgive us, folks, for impinging upon your valuable time with this little family do.' Small wonder that Baptism has not been seen as important." [9] CW-7 attempts to correct this by making Baptism more significant liturgically. It is placed in the context of the Chief Service of Word and Sacrament. This also restores the classical equilibrium between the word proclaimed, conversion in faith enacted through initiation, and the eucharistic celebration of all of this.

The universality of Baptism is maintained by not providing separate rites for the baptisms of infants and adults. There is no such thing as "infant baptism" or "adult baptism." There is only "one baptism for the forgiveness of sins." With one or two variants, the same rite can be used with young children and with adults.

The baptismal liturgy should be celebrated at periodic festivals. The rhythm of the congregation's activity year might determine when these festivals would be held, but there are certain days which are especially appropriate for Baptism for historical and theological reasons: Easter, Pentecost, Epiphany. The Easter Vigil is the time *par excellence* for Christian initiation. It underscores the relationship between the initiates dying and rising in Christ and the church's commemoration of his passover from death to life. But the Vigil also underscores the cosmic dimensions of Christian initiation. Aidan Kavanagh writes:

> When the Easter vigil 'speaks' about initiation, it does so in terms of a veritable evangelization of the cosmos. Fire, wind, wax, bees, light and darkness, water, oil, nakedness, bread, wine, aromas, tough and graceful words and gestures: all these stand as a context without which what

happens to one entering corporate faith in Jesus Christ dead and rising is only partially perceptible. The being and acts of Christ himself can even become constricted without regular paschal access to the full sweep of God's purpose that was being revealed long before the incarnation occurred. Because the discipline of Christian initiation is impoverished without regular access to the full paschal sweep of God's intents and accomplishments in Jesus Christ, the church becomes less than it is and may be, and so does the world.[10]

Consideration might also be given to a baptismal festival on one of the so-called "green" Sundays when the hymns, the propers and the sermon can all focus on Baptism. Propers are listed on p. 17 of CW-7.

The new liturgy tries to recover the richness of biblical imagery pertaining to Baptism. A comparison of orders currently used in the American Lutheran churches with Luther's two Orders of Baptism (1523 and 1526) will suffice to demonstrate how much of this imagery has been lost. One might compare Luther's famous *Sintflutgebet* ("flood prayer") on p. 3 of CW-7 with the Prayer of Thanksgiving on p. 27. These prayers draw reference to the waters of the creation, of the flood, of the Exodus, and of the Jordan as "types" of Baptism. Water is here seen as a symbol of new life, of destruction and death, and of purification. These images help to explain what Baptism is and connect Baptism in the church with the "types" of Baptism in salvation history.

The new liturgy gives the congregation more overt participation in the baptismal action. The people join verbally in the renunciation and confession; lay persons present the candidates, welcome the newly baptized into the fellowship, and present the white garment and the lighted candle.

The new liturgy gives explicit liturgical expression to the role of the Holy Spirit through the laying on of hands, the invocation of the indwelling gift of the Spirit, and the anointing with the oil of chrismation as a sign of the "seal of the Spirit." This restores the "two moments" of initiation referred to in some New Testament texts. In Acts 2:38, Peter exhorted his listeners to "repent, and be baptized every one of you in the name of Jesus Christ for the forgiveness of your sins; and you shall receive the gift of the Holy Spirit." According to Titus 3:5, we are saved "not because of deeds done by us in righteousness, but in virtue of his own mercy, by the washing of regeneration and renewal in the Holy Spirit." It is not necessary to see here two distinct rites; but it is clear that initiation in the New Testament was "by water and the Spirit." The earliest extant baptismal liturgies (such as that in the *Apostolic Tradition* of St. Hippolytus, A.D. 215) provide specific post-baptismal prayers invoking the Spirit on the newly baptized to accompany the laying on of hands. There is also a post-baptismal anointing in the *Apostolic Tradition*. These post-baptismal ceremonies mark the solemn public conclusion of the water-baptism, which was performed in relative privacy due to the candidates nudity. They are the substance and original context of what later came to be called confirmation.

The Greeks and Romans anointed themselves for athletic exercise. Oil also accompanied bathing in the ancient world, just as we today would use soap when washing. But the origins of the Christian use of oil are to be found in the anointing of kings and priests in the Old Testament. St. Ambrose identified this baptismal anointing as a kind of ordination and coronation: "that thou mayest become a chosen generation, priestly, precious: for we are all anointed with spiritual grace unto the kingdom of God." [11] Tertullian simply pointed out that the name "Christ means, "the Anointed One," and that we become "little Christs" by sharing in his anointing.

The signation came to be identified with the chrismation. The origins of marking a Christian with the sign of the cross go back to the Hebrew *taw* which was used as a brand to show ownership. In Ezekiel 9:4 the *taw* was marked on the

foreheads of the faithful who groaned over the abominations
committed in Jerusalem. Christians saw in this a prophetic
sign that the power of the cross of Christ would save them
from eschatological destruction. In Revelation 7:3 no destruction takes place until the servants of God have been "sealed"
on the forehead. The "seal" suggests a branding, a designation of God's own possessions. It is a promise that he will
claim his own at the day of redemption. Whenever and
wherever the sign of the cross is used in Christian devotion
it is a reminder of the eschatological salvation for which we
were set apart and sealed in our Baptism.

The use of the lighted candle and the white garment ritualize the ongoing dimensions of Baptism. The white garment
is a symbol of "putting on Christ," being covered with his
righteousness. The lighted candle is a sign of Christian presence in the world, faith experience being turned into concrete acts of ministry and prayer.

The celebration of Baptism in the context of the eucharistic
liturgy enables the progression of initiation to move from font
to altar within one service. There are no compelling theological reasons to prohibit infant communion. The Eastern
churches still practice it, and infant communion was practiced
in the West until the end of the Middle Ages. It was finally
stopped because of over-zealous scrupulosity concerning the
elements (i.e. infants unable to swallow the host, fear that
the precious blood might be spilled) rather than a genuine
concern that infants are not the proper subjects to receive
communion. But even if, for pastoral reasons, infant communion is not practiced, the progression from font to altar
suggests that the fellowship of the Lord's Supper is the *goal*
of Christian intiation. The parents and sponsors of young children will commune, and the children will at least be given a
blessing—at the Baptismal Eucharist and also at subsequent
Eucharists until such time as they can also partake of the
Lord's Supper.

The new liturgy gives clearer expression to the relationship between Baptism and the church, i.e. through the gesture of welcome spoken by the congregation at the end of the rite. In Holy Baptism God enlarges the communion of the church. But his adoption of news sons and daughters does not only affect them individually; it also affects the whole family of God. The church needs the presence of new Christians in its midst and needs to go through the Liturgy of Holy Baptism in order to be reminded of its own need for ongoing conversion and transformation in Christ.

The Importance of Ritual Actions

The new Liturgy of Holy Baptism is ceremonially fuller than previous Lutheran baptismal rites have been since the 16th century, although it is not as full as the pre-Reformation orders. But it at least restores to Baptism its character as a rite of initiation.

Like other rites of initiation, it deals concretely and symbolically with the human body. Only in this case it is God who acts in, with, and through the body as it is dunked in water, greased with oil, clothed in a white robe, and fed with the bread of life and the wine of eternal salvation. Most remarkably of all, God puts his Spirit into these bodies (Ezek. 36:27) so that the body becomes the "temple of the Holy Spirit" (1 Cor. 6:19). There is no more concrete way that God could deal with an individual than through his body. Nor is it such a strange thing for God to do. He's done it before: all the fullness of God inhabited a body, the body of Christ. And we become members of that body through Holy Baptism.

The actions performed on the body speak louder than words. The use of such symbolic objects as the oil of chrismation, the white garment, and the lighted candle help to ritualize the reality of Baptism. The oil should preferably be olive mixed with myron or perfume or scent of some kind. The white garment put on adults might be an alb or surplice which might then reinforce the symbolism of this vestment which is usually worn by the pastor and other worship leaders. The baptismal candle should be a miniature paschal candle, which will reinforce the relationship between Baptism and Easter.

But the most important material in the baptismal rite is the *water*. It is a cosmic symbol of life, of death and destruction, and of cleansing and purification. In the sacrament it also represents the world itself, the matter of creation. Blessing it in the baptismal liturgy has a truly cosmic and redemptive significance. By giving thanks over the water, we proclaim it to be what God intended it to be from the very beginning: his gift to us and our means of communion with him. This is the purpose in giving thanks over any material element (see 1 Tim. 4:4-5).

There is an ecological implication in this eucharistic recognition that the matter of creation is a "theatre of grace." The sacraments have been called "the economy of salvation," which suggests an eco-system in which everything is related to everything else. If this is not seen in the water of Baptism, it is doubtful that it will be seen at all. To be sure, the water or any other material elements is not self-evidently the gift of God and the means of communion with him. That is why we give thanks over it: to proclaim what it is by divine intention and promise. In the act of *eucharistia* we are able to move beyond the post-Reformation privatizing of grace and learn, as Joseph Sittler suggests, "that nature and grace, perception, experience, and wonder, the creation as the habitat of our bodies, and the divine redemption as the Word of God to our spirits, must all be held together in thought as indeed they occur in fact." [12]

Sacramental theology affirms that nature is a given arena of the encounter with the grace of the triune God. The eucharistic prayer over the water, as over the bread and wine, draws upon the rhetoric of recollection, reenactment, and extention to celebrate the creative, redeeming, sanctifying work of God. The praise of his mighty acts leads to remembrance

(anamnesis); invocation *(epiclesis)* is the extension and concrete application of the remembered actuality and promise of
what God has done and will do. The Spirit who moved over
the waters of chaos is invoked to make the water of the font a
"water of cleansing," to "wash away the sins of all who enter
it, and bring them forth as inheritors of your glorious kingdom" (CW-7, p. 35). By water, Word, and Spirit the new
Christian is plunged into the past, present, and future of God's
creative, redemptive, sanctifying work.

This is powerful imagery, and the only way to let this evo-
cation of God's grace through water speak is to use the matter at hand in abundance. "To baptize" means "to immerse."
St. Ambrose noticed the symbolic connection between being
dipped in the font and being buried in the tomb with Christ.
Would a casual onlooker receive the same impression from
our practice? Sprinkling is as symbolically minimal and im-
potent as the use of little wafers of bread and thimbles of
wine in Holy Communion. We will simply have to use more
water.

Suggestion I: Immersion is a compelling way to perform Baptisms. What would be the logistical requirements of such a
practice? The ancient church buildings contained what we
might call semi-private "bath houses" adjacent to the sanc-
tuaries called "baptisteries." This provided a modicum of
modesty for the stark naked candidates who were being led
into the waters of rebirth. The ancient church orders prescribed that female ministers (i.e. deaconesses) baptize adult
female candidates.

Suggestion II: Locate the font near the church entrance. This
will allow for grander processions to and from the font during the Baptismal Liturgy, and there's always something compelling about a well-done parade. The font will also remind
the faithful as they enter and leave the church that the whole
Christian life is nothing but a living out of baptism. Leave

blessed water in the font, and encourage the people to dip their hand in it and trace on their bodies the sign of the cross with which they were marked and sealed forever. This will encourage the use of the sign of the cross elsewhere in Christian devotion: i.e. at the invocation, at the end of the Creed, at the "blessed is he" of the Sanctus, at the reception of Holy Communion, and at the benediction.

Leadership in the Affirmation of the Baptismal Covenant

To be assigned to the history of Jesus Christ in Holy Baptism is also to be assigned to the community of Jesus' people. God's purpose throughout salvation history has been to "call, gather, enlighten, and sanctify" a people who shall be his own. This is the basis of the covenant between God and Israel, and between Christ and his church. Baptism makes a person a member of the covenant community. Any major transitions made in Christian life thereafter should be based on the transition made into Christian life once and for all in Holy Baptism. Whether completing post-baptismal catechesis, joining a new community of faith, or returning to active participation in the life and mission of the church after a period of neglect or lapse, the Christian should affirm the covenant God once made with him in Holy Baptism. This is the purpose of CW-8: *Affirmation of the Baptismal Covenant.* Multiple uses are foreseen for the use of this rite:

1. for what has traditionally been called the rite of confirmation of those young people who have been prepared through the pastoral and educational ministry of the church to make public profession of their faith and commit themselves to the life and mission of the church in a more responsible way; [13]

2. for receiving new members into the congregation by letter of transfer from sister congregations or by instruction from other denominations; and

3. for restoring the lapsed to active membership in the congregation.
4. A general use is foreseen for those who desire to renew their commitment to the life and mission of the church as a result of some new insight, experience, or opportunity.

This rite should be used in the context of the service of Holy Communion since participation in the eucharistic meal is the clearest means of expressing and celebrating the new covenant between God and man inaugurated by Jesus Christ.

Whenever possible, the Rite of Affirmation should be used in the context of the Liturgy of Holy Baptism. This will underscore the fact that all transitions in Christian life *are* made in reference to the primary transition *into* Christian life in the Sacrament of Holy Baptism. It will also bring out the implications of the ongoing dimension of baptismal living.

How to Do the Rite of Affirmation

1. When the Rite is *not* used in the context of a baptismal celebration
   - After the Hymn of the Day, a representative of the congregation (e.g. a member of the church council) presents those who are affirming their baptismal covenant. Various forms of presentation are provided, from which the appropriate one is selected.
   - The presiding minister extends a word of greeting and invites the candidates and the congregation to repeat the solemn profession of faith which was made at Holy Baptism.
   - The assisting minister leads the intercessory prayers. The intercessions (Prayer of the Church) for the day are included here.
   - The presiding minister asks the candidates if they intend to continue in the covenant God made with them in Holy Baptism. Each person answers individually, "I do, and I ask God to help and guide me."

- The presiding minister prays that the Holy Spirit, given to these persons at their Baptism, may increase the gifts of grace in them. When the Rite of Affirmation is used at Confirmation, the presiding minister lays hands on their heads individually and prays:

    N. the Father in heaven, for Jesus' sake, strengthen in you the gift of the Holy Spirit, to deepen your faith, to direct your life, to empower you for service, to give you patience in suffering, and to bring you to ever-lasting life.

    (In manual acts such as this, the presiding minister should have an acolyte available to hold his book so that his hands are free.)

- The presiding minister briefly addresses the candidates and extends to them the greeting of peace. They, in turn, carry the greeting of peace to the other members of the congregation.

- The Liturgy continues with the Offertory.

2. When the Affirmation is undertaken within the Liturgy of Holy Baptism

    - During the Hymn the candidates for baptism are brought to the font or to the front of the church by their parents and/or sponsors.

    - The sponsors present each candidate by name. If they can answer for themselves, the minister asks the candidates: "Do you desire to be baptized?" He then reminds the sponsors of their continuing responsibilities.

    - The representatives of the congregation present those who are affirming their baptismal covenant and the pre-siding minister extends a word of greeting to them.

    - The presiding minister invites the baptismal candidates, their parents and/or sponsors, the persons affirming their baptismal covenant, and the whole congregation to con-fess the faith of the church.

    - The assisting minister leads the intercessory prayers for

the baptized, for their parents and/or sponsors, and for those affirming the covenant of their Baptism. If the service up to now has been conducted in front of the congregation or at the altar, all process to the font during the intercessory prayers. It is no great difficulty to read the prayers while walking in solemn procession. It is even better to sing them as a litany. A simple reciting tone will suffice if no other music is available. A crucifer and acolytes with torches may lead the procession.

- At the font the presiding minister gives thanks over the water, thus consecrating it for its holy purpose. As he begins the prayer of thanksgiving an assisting minister may slowly pour the water into the font. At the invocation of the Holy Spirit ("Pour out your gracious Spirit . . .") it is also traditional to dip the paschal candle into the water three times—thus identifying this Baptism with the passover of Christ. (It's also a marvelous fertility symbol. Isn't the church made pregnant with the conception of these new children about to be born in the waters of the font?)
- The baptisms take place.
- A hymn (just a verse or two will suffice) is sung while the group at the font processes back to the front of the church.
- The newly baptized kneel and the presiding minister lays his hands on the head of each, invoking the indwelling gift of the Spirit.
- He then marks the sign of the cross on the forehead of each of the baptized using the oil prepared for this purpose. The white robe and the lighted candle are presented to the baptized by representatives of the congregation.
- The presiding minister addresses those making affirmation. He invites them to state their intention to continue in the covenant of their Baptism.
- Those making affirmation kneel; the presiding minister

prays for the renewed gift of the Spirit in all of them and lays his hands on each one individually.

- The minister directs all the people who have been involved in the rites to face the congregation. He presents those who have been baptized and those who have affirmed their baptismal covenant. The congregation welcomes them into the fellowship of this particular family of God.
- The ministers share the sign of peace with the baptized, with their parents and/or sponsors, with those who have affirmed the baptismal covenant. They give the sign of peace to one another and to other members of the congregation.
- The service continues with the Offertory. It is appropriate for the newly baptized, their parents and sponsors, and for those who have affirmed their baptismal covenant to offer the bread and wine for the Eucharist. They may provide it out of their own larder.

It remains to be seen how effective CW-7 and CW-8 will be in renewing our practice of Christian initiation. Rites remain just words on a page until they are *enacted* in a worshiping community. From the limited use they have received so far, however, it seems that they have the capability of making an experiential impact on the congregation. This is a step in the right directon if we are to take seriously the assertion that the rites of Christian initiation constitute the charter of the church's existence. The effective performance of the Liturgy of Holy Baptism, together with the Affirmation of the Baptismal Covenant, may do more than preaching, and teaching to impress upon the church what it means to be the eschatological body of Christ.

4

Actions in Worship

Meaningful movement: liturgical choreography

Seeing has been a neglected sense in Protestant worship because the emphasis on *hearing* the Word tended to blot out anything that might intrude on the attention given to the Word. Yet the liturgy is a drama, and a drama requires seeing as well as hearing.

There are obvious dangers in reviving the concept of liturgy as drama. Alexander Schmemann points out that the mysteriological concepts imported into the church during and after the time of Constantine tended to make the liturgy a "cult-drama" which re-enacted "the central actions in a given event, as a communion in this event, as a reception of its meaning, power, and special efficacy."[1] The dramatic qualities of the liturgy were exploited for all they were worth in the medieval commentaries on the Mass, often using the most fanciful allegorical explanations.[2] It is no wonder that some Lutherans are reticent to talk about the liturgy in dramatic terms. For them "action" is another word for "work," in the sense of an *opus operatum*.[3] This concept of the cult-drama carries the impression that the doing of the ritual has an effect on God.

While eschewing any kind of mechanistic (indeed magical) understanding of the liturgy, we may still point out that the dramatic aspect of the liturgy would be evident to any

casual onlooker. It would seem that one of the persons in
the assembly is playing Jesus and the rest are his disciples.
The sermon is still delivered from a kind of "mountain," i.e.
the pulpit, and the Lord's Table still serves as a reminder of
the institution of the Lord's Supper in the Upper Room. It
is therefore important to consider the dramatic qualities of
worship. As Robert Jenson notes,

> The other arts occur in worship incidentally to its dra-
> matic character, and for the same reasons as they occur
> in the drama generally. This performance occupies a
> stage, and uses stage-settings, costumes, props, and above
> all rhythmically and melodiously intensified language.
> Therefore the poets, musicians, goldsmiths, painters, de-
> signers, architects, and all the troop of art are called in to
> work in the production. And if they are not, if the play
> is done in "everyday language" and in "modern dress"
> or rehearsal clothes, this too is an artistic device for a
> particular effect.[4]

Worship is drama because the liturgy is a ritual enactment
of the Gospel. The Gospel is a story, but it is not a mono-
log; it is dialogical and it calls for *response*. This accounts
for the dialogical character of the liturgy: the acclamations,
antiphons, versicles and responses. But as a drama, the sights
as well as the sounds of the liturgy will contribute toward
making the experience gripping or dull. There is no moment
in the liturgy which is visually unimportant.

Processions

Processions constitute the most visual moments in the
liturgy. The following processional moments may be noted:

1. *The Entrance Procession* with vocal and/or instrumental
   music establishes the clear beginning of the liturgy. It also
   serves to establish the character of the Liturgy as a hos-
   pitable, communal, prayerful activity. The ministers walk

through the assembly to the place of ministerial action. It is best if the choir is already in place so that they can lead the singing. The ministers bow to the altar and the presiding minister (why not?) also bows to the people. They go directly to their seats. Objects carried in the procession (books, cross, candles, banners) are put in their places.

2. *The Gospel procession* may be used on major festivals. During the singing of the Alleluia Verse the crucifer and two acolytes with torches lead the procession into the center of the nave. The lector who has read the first and second lessons carries the Bible or Lectionary and the presiding or assisting minister who is to read the Gospel follows after him. When the procession reaches its destination the crucifer stops, turns around, and faces the minister who will read the Gospel. The acolytes stand on each side of the book facing in. The lector faces the minister and holds the book open to the Gospel reading.

(1) Crucifer
(2) Acolytes
(3) Lector
(4) Minister

At the end of the reading the lector and minister step aside to allow the crucifer and acolytes to lead the procession back through the assembly. The book is returned to its place and the ministers return to their chairs.

3. *The Offertory procession* may be done in a simpler or a more complex way.
   (a) Simple offertory: the ushers gather the money gifts of the people. With two representatives of the people bearing the gifts of bread and wine, they bring all the gifts forward. Assisting ministers receive the gifts and take them to the presiding minister at the altar.

(b) Elaborate offertory: all the people come forward with their gifts The acolytes may stand at the chancel entrance holding plates to receive the money gifts while the assisting ministers receive the gifts of bread and wine. Ushers may be needed to help direct the people back to their seats via some side aisle.

The presiding minister in public view

Among the presidential actions to be noted for their visual effect are:

1. *Greeting the people.* Look at them, gesture to them. Christian liturgy is *person*-oriented.

2. *Invitation to prayer.* Observe a moment of silence so that the people have time to get themselves into a frame of mind for prayer. The minister's attitude toward silence will eventually influence the people's. If he is embarrassed by silence, they will be also. If he jealously guards it as a time of recollection, so will they.

3. *The Greeting of peace.* The president sets the example by greeting the other ministers and some members of the congregation. If the presiding minister communicates a naturalness in greeting the people with the sign of peace, they will eventually respond in kind.

4. *Receiving the communion vessels and the gifts.* Communion vessels should be stored on a side table until the beginning of the offertory, when they are brought to the altar by acolytes or an assistant minister. The chalice is placed on the center of the corporal, the paten in front of it. The extra bread and wine are placed behind the chalice, the bread to the left corner of the corporal and the cruets or flagons of wine to the right. Arranging the vessels is a purely utilitarian act. There is no need for the people to watch the setting of the table. So the assisting minister might stand across the altar (if it is free-standing) from the presiding minister during the reception and

arranging of the gifts. The gifts of money might be placed at the extreme end of the altar or they may be removed elsewhere.

Altar Mensa

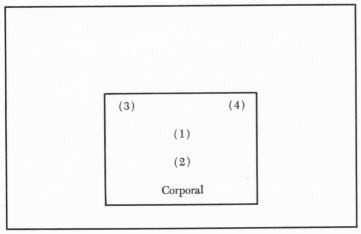

(1) Chalice
(2) Paten
(3) Bread
(4) Wine

It is customary for the presiding minister to wash his hands after the offertory. A small bowl with a cruet of water and a finger towel may be stored on a side credence table for this purpose. They can be brought to the presiding minister by an acolyte. (This is called the *lavabo*.)

5. *The Great Thanksgiving.* The presiding minister should extend his hands in the classical gesture of prayer. This as appropriate for all presidential prayers, but especially for the great eucharistic prayer. This means that the presiding minister must have his hands free. An assisting minister or an acolyte can always hold the book or sheet of paper if there is no place to set it.

During the words over the bread, the minister takes the bread in his hands; during the words over the cup the minister takes the cup in his hands. During the epiclesis the minister extends his hands over the elements in a gesture of blessing. During the doxology he elevates the elements in a grand gesture so that they may be seen by all. (On the elevation in Lutheran practice, see chapter 1.)

6. *The breaking of bread.* The presiding minister breaks the main loaf or the large host. Then an assisting minister may help him break the rest of the bread into small pieces. During this action the *Agnus Dei* may be sung and the acolytes may bring to the altar any other vessels which are needed for the administration.

7. *The Holy Communion.* The presiding minister communes himself first, then his assistants and servers. During the communion it is important to pay attention to the attitude of reverence and to the person-to-person element in the administration. Ministers and communicants make contact with their eyes, facial expressions, and by touch of hand.

8. *Clearing the table.* As soon as all have communed the communion blessing should be given. The vessels can be removed from the altar and returned to the credence table during the singing of the post-communion song, chant or hymn. What remains in the chalice after the administration should be consumed, and the chalice cleaned by pouring a little water into it. (This is called the *ablution.*) The corporal, which is likely to contain crumbs, may be folded inward so that the crumbs do not fall on the floor. The concern here is simply to maintain a reverential care.

9. *Closing prayer.* Observe a long period of silence after the post-communion prayer and before the benediction. This is the time for final meditation, not after the dismissal.

10. *Exit.* Depart after the dismissal as deliberately as possible. The exit should serve to underscore the fact that the Liturgy of the Eucharistic Meal is ended; the Liturgy of

Mission is beginning. The benediction and dismissal serves as a type of the "great commission."

The lector in public view

Lectors need to be rehearsed for their approach to and departure from the ambo (lectern) and book, as well as for the readings themselves. They should pause before beginning to read to allow the congregation time to settle down and prepare to hear the readings.

The lector should stand at the ambo and read from the Bible itself, or else from an impressively-bound lectionary. To read from flimsy bulletin inserts does not accord the proclamation of the Word the ritual moment it deserves. The Word should be seen as well as heard.

The acolyte in public view

Acolytes are not liturgical decorations. In too many places the acolytes do not do enough during the service, and often this is because they are too young to carry out meaningful tasks. Acolytes should be older youths or even adults. There is nothing demeaning about serving the Lord's people at his table. These are some things for acolytes to do:

- Carry the cross, torches, books and thurible (incense pot) in processions.
- Convey the communion vessels from the credence table to the altar at the offertory.
- Receive the offering plates from the ushers or other gifts from the people.
- Attend the presiding minister for the *lavabo*.
- During the communion see that each minister is adequately supplied with bread and wine.
- Assist the ministers in clearing the table after the communion.

Note: it is not necessary to light or extinguish candles as a part of the service. Except for the light-ceremony *(lucer-narium)* at Vespers, it is a purely utilitarian act. Candles may be lit before the service starts and extinguished after the people leave.

The Cantor in public view

The term "cantor" is used to designate the person who leads the congregational singing. This person may be the choir director or a member of the choir, but not of necessity. These are some things for the cantor to do:

1. *Direct the people in singing hymns,* especially new or difficult hymns, and especially if the choir or instruments are providing an "obligato." The cantor can stand in front of the people in order to effectively bring them in on cue and engender enthusiasm.

2. *Lead the singing of psalms.* The following method has proven useful in reviving congregational psalm-singing. The cantor sings a simple, one-line antiphon: it is repeated initially by all. Then the cantor sings the verses of the psalm and the congregation sings the antiphon at the end of each verse. This is the method used in *The Psalmody for the Day,* published for the three-year lectionary. If the choir sings the verses of the psalm, the cantor can still bring the people in on the antiphon.

   Uses of psalmody:

   (a) The Responsorial Psalm between the first and second lessons. This is the *prescribed* psalm for the day: it is usually correlated with the first lesson as a meditative reflection on it. Practically, it also breaks up the readings. What could be more monotonous than several readings back to back?

   (b) *The Psalmody for the Day* also provides psalms of seasonal character to use as introits or entrance hymns, and psalms to be sung during communion.

   (c) Introits and graduals may continue to be used with the liturgy in the SBH or TLH.

3. *Rehearse the people through new music,* perhaps before the service begins.

The Usher in public view

The usher is essentially a host. His demeanor and attitude can affect the way people feel about being in church. These are some things for ushers to do:

- Help people find their seats as they enter the sanctuary, especially after the seats have begun to fill up.
- Provide the people with whatever liturgical material is needed for the service.
- Assist people during times of movement such as the offertory procession and the communion.
- Gather the offerings of the people.
- Know what is happening in the service so that any worshiper can be helped who seems lost in the Service Book or unsure of where to go during congregational movement.
- Keep a low profile; avoid military precision. Lady ushers may help the men to act more like hosts and less like honor guards.

Places of Action

The entrance rite is conducted from the ministers' *chairs.* The chair has been, of late, an unused piece of liturgical furniture. Yet the sometimes over-whelming size of clergy chairs in our parishes suggests that it has some symbolic value as a seat of teaching authority. (Remember the phrase *ex cathedra?* Bishops in the ancient church sometimes used to preach from their chairs.) The presidential chair should be located in some prominent, visible place. Chairs of the assisting ministers can be placed on either side of it. In Example A below, the chairs are located behind the altar on a raised platform. In Example B, they are located at the side of the altar.

86 *Actions in Worship*

Example A:
The chancels of many existing churches can be rebuilt by moving the altar away from the wall and placing the ministers' chairs on the old platform.

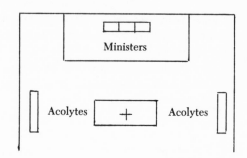

Example B:
The chancels of many existing churches can be rebuilt by moving the altar away from the wall, locating it on a new raised platform in the center of the chancel, putting the choir behind the altar, and placing the ministers' chairs on the side wall between the choir and congregation.

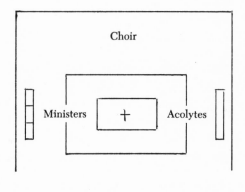

The Liturgy of the Word is conducted at the *ambo*. The ambo is a reading desk or a reading stand large enough to hold a big book. Most churches have a lectern and a pulpit. The first two lessons can be read from the lectern, the Gospel and Sermon from the pulpit. If there is only one ambo, all the lessons and the sermon should be proclaimed from it. The ambo gives the Word its own place of attention. The entire Service of the Word (CW-5) can be conducted from the ambo, except perhaps for the final prayers which can be read from the chairs. (The Gospel, of course, may be carried in procession and be proclaimed from the center of the assembly.)

The Intercessions may be prayed from the chairs or the ambo. This does not prohibit bids and petitions coming from the midst of the assembly.

The eucharistic meal is celebrated at the *altar*. The table is needed to serve the meal; it is used only when the Eucharist is celebrated.

The people should always face toward the place of action if at all possible. During processions they can follow the cross. If the Gospel is proclaimed from the center aisle, they should face there. If there is a Baptism at the back of the church, they should turn and face the font. Do you get the feeling that pews get in the way? Moveable chairs function much more flexibly.

Meaningful words: liturgical speech

We are generally more at ease with words and speech than with gestures and movement. In our increasingly rationalistic culture we are embarrassed by body language. As verbiage in worship mushrooms, our gestures become smaller and more mechanical. Ironically, words deprived of action lose their authority. We learned that from the social activism of the 1960s. Robert Jenson reminds us that

> As worship becomes prosy, its utterance loses those articulations by which it can free us from the status quo of our lives and world, by which it can function as promise. Then the specific futures once held out as hope and promise become mere ideals, and our realization of them mere tasks. Our worship becomes a moralistic exercise.[5]

This prosaic tendency was especially noticeable in the Reformed tradition. Lutherans have usually preferred the concise statements of the classical Latin collects. Since the Words of Institution were generally used alone, apart from the context of a full eucharistic prayer, the Reformed tendency to compose lengthy, didactic eucharistic prayers was avoided (although verbosity was usually made up for in the sermon and in the General Prayer). Many experimental services of the 1960s, even in Lutheran circles, succumbed to the homiletizing impulse as they attempted to demythologize traditional concepts. They usually succeeded in turning worship into what Jenson has called "a rather dull and inefficient sermon."

The corrective to this is to *curb the tongue*. Our verbal language is neither our deepest nor our most effective means of communication. Liturgy is more than words on a page. It involves the totality of human expression. As we allow other means of communication to expand, our use of words must contract. The result will not be a de-emphasis on the importance of the spoken word, but a liberation of the spoken word to do its job.

The word in prayer

There are opportunities for "spontaneous prayer" in the new Communion Service (CW-2) especially in the confession of sins and the general intercessions. Prayer petitions should be brief, specific, and literate:

Examples for the confession of sins:

- Our hatred which divides us nation from nation, race from race, class from class, family from family, we confess to the Lord. R/ Forgive us Lord.
- Our covetous desires to possess what is not our own, we confess to the Lord. R/
- Our greed which exploits the labors of other people and lays waste to the earth, we confess to the Lord. R/

  Examples for the intercessions:

- For the church throughout the world, and especially for this parish, that it may be faithful to its mission: Lord, in your mercy, R/ Hear our prayer.
- For the leaders of the church, for N. our chief pastor, N. our bishop, and N. our dean, that they may know and do your will: Lord, in your mercy. R/

- For our nation and all nations, and for persons in positions of authority, especially N. our president, N. our governor, and N. our mayor, that they may govern wisely and we may prosper under them: Lord, in your mercy. R/
- For those who are hospitalized or ill, especially N. N., that they may know the healing power of the Holy Spirit and be strengthened in this time of their affliction: Lord, in your mercy, R/
- For those who have gone before us marked with the sign of faith, especially N. N., that they may find in your presence light, refreshment, and peace: Lord, in your mercy, R/

There are things which should *not* be done in prayer.

1. *Don't hammer away at sinfulness.* The modern person doesn't see himself as especially poor or relentlessly miserable. We may be saints and sinners at the same time, but the constant stress on the sinful side of *redeemed* humanity plays down the work God has already done through his gracious Spirit. The Spirit's presence and activity in the church must count for something. As James White suggests, "Western Christianity has probably overdone its stress on the element of contrition for man's sins." [6]

2. *Don't be dogmatic or homiletic.* We may bring any petitions we want before God. It is even possible for different Christians in the same assembly to pray for diametrically opposite causes. But we have to maintain a stance of humility: "We do not even know how we ought to pray as we ought but the Spirit himself intercedes with us with sighs too deep for words" (Rom. 8:26). There are limits to our knowledge of God and his will as well as to our own words, so we should avoid telling God what to do and limit ourselves just to asking for his grace and favor, so that we may do his will.

3. *Don't be verbose.* In this day of instant impact through

mass media we cannot afford to be straying travellers from the days of Gutenberg's printed page.

The word in proclamation

In the new rite it is possible to make comments on the theme of the day before the reading of the First Lesson. This is not a place for another sermon, nor is it time to be didactic. It is rather an opportunity to set the stage for the celebration by proclaiming the central meaning of the day's liturgy as it is reflected in the readings.

Examples:

Holy Trinity: (General for the Festival) We Christians speak of God because we cannot be silent. We have experienced his Fatherly care which provides for our needs, his brotherly love which sacrificed itself for us and for our salvation, and his sanctifying grace which restores us to himself. We confess and celebrate the mystery of the Holy Trinity, not because we know so much about God as he is in himself, but because we have experienced his creative, redemptive, sanctifying work in our own lives; and we praise his Holy Name, not as we ought, but as we are able. Let us be attentive to the Word of God.

Second Sunday after Pentecost (Year A): As we begin the half year of the church, our readings take up the theme of obedience: obedience which is a response to God's love and faithfulness; obedience which is an act of justifying faith in Christ Jesus; obedience to a Master who does not make us submissive to his power, but who teaches us as one with authority. Let us be attentive to the Word of God.

Special consideration should be given to the spoken word of the lay lector. The lector has an awesome task: to stand before the congregation and proclaim what is written in God's Word. That Word has to be proclaimed clearly so that it may be heard and understood by all. This is no time to stammer, stumble, mumble or mispronounce biblical names.

The lector need not resort to a "preacher's tone" when he or she is reading; nor need the lector resort to dramatization. The model for good reading is not the heavy actor or actress but the news broadcaster who reads evenly, audibly, and clearly with only the most subtle inflections and modulations of the voice.

An Experiment

Go through the whole liturgy using only gestures and one word for each section to express the meaning of each part of the service. For example, the Greeting—extend arms toward people—hello, welcome, peace; Prayer for the Day—close hands, then uplift them—pray; Announcement of the Day—finger to ear—hear, listen, attend; do the same for the Intercessions, Offertory, Eucharistic Prayer (one word allowed for each section: preface, sanctus, recital of salvation history, words over the bread, words over the cup, anamnesis, epiclesis, intercession, doxology), Lord's Prayer, Breaking of bread (are any words needed here at all?), Communion, Post-Communion, Benediction.

The purpose of this exercise is to increase understanding of the progression of the liturgy, see the importance of nonverbal communication (body language), and make words count. Becoming familiar with the arts of dance and mime might help worship leaders learn body carriage, posture, movement and gesture so that they can walk, move and gesture with beauty, dignity and grace.

Meaningful space: liturgical environment

Liturgical action depends on the architectural space for worship. It is by now a classical architectural motto that "form follows function." This has not always been the case. Often in the past would-be liturgical reform floundered because the church buildings got in the way of the liturgy. Old forms could not accommodate new functions. As E. A. Sovik writes:

> . . . architecture is a more influential factor in the life of society than most people suppose. The incompleteness of the Reformation in terms of architecture was no doubt the result of the longevity of architecture. Buildings stand, and are not easily removed or changed.[7]

This does not necessarily mean that we must tear down old buildings and start from scratch. It is easier just to alter the internal structure and shape of the space used for worship. Sometimes it is possible to create a workable space for worship just by rearranging the furniture and making a judicious use of banners, lights and screens.

Caution must be observed in altering the worship space. It is necessary to know your space, because each space has its own unique character. It is necessary to know what you want the space to do and then to determine if the space is capable of doing it. It is advisable to call in architectural advisors. Sometimes a space may be made to work without altering it in any significant way. The following concerns ought to be kept in mind.

A building should allow for a variety of uses. In considering the creation of a workable worship space the *whole* space must be taken into account. Liturgical action should not be restricted just to a sanctuary.

One way to allow for a variety of uses is to focus on different places in the building. It is neither necessary nor desirable to be moving things around all the time. That can be quite disorienting and unsettling for the people. They have to know where they are and be comfortable with their surroundings. The better alternative is to focus on places of liturgical action by drawing attention to what is happening at those places through the use of symbolic objects. For example:

• Focus on the presidential *chair* by placing the cross and/ or banners next to it. Since the people will be following the entrance procession they will get the point that the chair is the first place of action if the processional cross goes to it.

• Focus on the *ambo* by placing the torches on either side of it. The torches will also accompany the Bible or lectionary ൧ it is carried in the Gospel procession for the proclamation of the Gospel. Wherever the candles go, to the middle of the nave or to the pulpit, they will attract the attention of the people to that place of action.

• Focus on the baptismal *font* by lighting the paschal candle and placing it next to the font on occasions when there are baptisms. (During the paschal season, of course, the candle will be near the pulpit; but it can be carried in procession to the font if there are baptisms during the paschal season.)

• Focus on the *altar* by bringing the vessels and gifts to it at the offertory. If incense is used, the censing of the altar might await the offertory. That would also highlight the altar as the place of liturgical action. Prior to this the incense might be carried in procession to cense the people and the ministers during the entrance. Then it might be carried in the Gospel procession to cense the book before the reading of the Gospel.

A second way to provide for a variety of uses is to *move the people* from place to place. Some services call for liturgical acts which take place "outside the sanctuary." For example, the Palm Sunday service begins with the blessing and distribution of palms. This can be done in some place of assembly other than the "sanctuary" such as the church porch, the narthex, the fellowship hall, or even the parking lot. The Easter Vigil begins outside the church door with the lighting and blessing of the new fire and the paschal candle. If the congregation is small in number, the people can be invited to stand around the font during the baptisms at the vigil. This is an effective way for the congregation to renew its baptismal covenant. In small congregations the people can also be invited to come forward at the Offertory and stand around the altar during the Eucharistic Prayer and the Communion.

On some occasions it might be possible to transfer the situation which might pertain in a "house church" to the institutional church building. Different rooms can be used for different acts of the liturgical drama: a school-room (synagogue) for the Liturgy of the Word, a bathroom (baptistery) for the Liturgy of Holy Baptism, and a dining room ("altar room") for the Liturgy of the Eucharistic Meal.

A via media between focusing on different places and objects of liturgical action and moving the people to where the action is, is to keep the people relatively stationary but locate the ambo, font, and altar in different areas of the worship hall. This is an effective way of defining different functional spaces. For example, the ambo or pulpit might be at the front of the hall, the font at the back of the hall near the entrance, and the altar in the middle of the seating area. This will form an axis between ambo, font, and altar. It will necessitate processions from place to place for different parts of the liturgy. It will also create a sense of active involvement in the liturgical action, because everything isn't happening "up there on the stage."

It is important to establish a rapport between the people and the presiding minister. The worship space should be designed to facilitate this.

• In terms of *architecture:* there should be no barriers between the people and the presiding minister. Except perhaps when he is at the font, the pastor should be able to make eye-contact with the congregation.

• In terms of creating a *liturgical environment:* everything depends on the presiding minister's sense of personal presence. He must be consciously aware of his conspicuous role in the worship space and bring to bear the demeanor which communicates his belief in God's presence among his people in Word and Sacrament. A proper liturgical demeanor is genuine naturalness of gesture and movement, not artificial folksiness or stiff formality.

• In terms of getting *people's attention:* don't burden them with a lot of books and papers with which to fumble. The less the people have in their hands, the better. Let them cultivate the use of their ears, eyes and other senses. Most Lutherans know from memory the words and music of their liturgy. If the material is familiar, the people don't need service books. Nor do they need lectionary sheets if the lectors read slowly and clearly. A simple psalm antiphon can be repeated after the cantor sings it just by hearing it. All the people really need are the hymns. Both ministers and people should realize that ritual gestures are meaningful only when they are recalled spontaneously.

Decorating the worship space[8]

The designs used in the worship space should fit the church building and the worship area. Banners, crosses, candles, etc. should be proportionate to the size of the room. This is determined by their visibility. The objects must be seen by all the people in the room. It is better to err on the side of bigness in designing these objects. But care must be taken that they do not obscure the focal points: chair, ambo, altar.

The designs should fit the liturgical experience of the day or season. Sameness is the easiest thing to do. It is easy to always order two bunches of flowers; but it takes a little time and effort to plan other arrangements. Banners, vestments, paraments and even floral arrangements should be designed to fit the theme of the day or season.

The designs should be imaginative. Here are some hints:

1. *Flowers* do not always have to be at the altar. They can be anywhere: next to the ambo, by the font, in the midst of the people or even in the people's hands. They don't always have to be on a stand; they can be hung, placed on a pedestal

or shelf, or put on the floor. They don't always have to be arranged by florists or members of the altar guild; they can be arranged by children from the bunches that they pick on the way to church (from their own gardens of course!).

2. *Candles* do not always have to be in metal holders; they can be stuck into bowls or held in people's hands. They don't always have to be arranged symmetrically: they can be placed at one end of the altar, or on the floor as tall guards next to the altar, or clustered around some other focal point. There doesn't always have to be two or six candles; there might be one or thirty. (Why not have seven votive lights on the altar on Pentecost to symbolize the seven-fold gifts of the Spirit?)

3. *Banners* don't always have to be three feet by six feet: they can be eight inches by eight feet or three feet by thirty feet. They don't always have to be hanging from a pole: they can hang on the wall or from the rafters. They can be made of burlap, felt, silk, wool, plastic, wood or metal. "Banner" is a concept, not a material.

Finally, the designs should be uncluttered. One can have too much of a good thing and thereby dissipate the whole effect of the liturgical decorations. It's better to have a few things out at a time, but change them frequently, than to have everything out at once and leave them in a state of near-permanence. In this way the designs can be changed to help highlight the seasons and festivals of the church year. In all this the designers should exercise good taste. That's what creativity largely is. That's also why an aesthetic sense can be considered a gift. Those who have this gift should be encouraged to use it for the edification of the people of God.

5

Coordination in Worship

The Worship Team: lay involvement and its rationale

There has been in recent years a new emphasis on the priesthood of believers. This has grown out of the liturgical movement's concern to revitalize the sense of community in the church through corporate worship. Liturgical renewal is inseparable from church renewal in all its aspects.

Luther attacked the Mass as a "priestly monopoly." When he denied the sacrifice-character of the Mass, he also rejected the so-called "indelible character" which was given to ordained priests to confect the sacrament (in the miracle of the transubstantiation) and to offer the sacrifice of the Mass. Instead, he emphasized the communion-character of the Mass, and with it the fact that the Mass belongs to the people of God. It is an act of corporate worship; therefore private masses could not be tolerated.

In reaction, Roman Catholic theologians after the Council of Trent emphasized the dignity of the ordained ministry and de-emphasized the role of the lay priesthood.

The liturgical movement of the 20th century has sought to mediate between these two extreme positions. It has affirmed what Luther taught about the general priesthood of the laity; but it has said that this need not deny the specific authority committed to the ordained ministry in the church to proclaim the Word and celebrate the sacraments. It has also suggested that the denial of any sacrificial content to the Mass or other forms of Christian worship empties even the lay priesthood of its essential content and character. This is because a priest is essentially one who offers sacrifice.

Alexander Schmemann writes that "Man was created priest of the world, the one who offers the world to God in a sacrifice of love and praise and who, through this eternal Eucharist, bestows the Divine love upon the world. . . ."[1] Because of man's sin and age-old rebellion, the job has not been done very well. In fact, only in Christ is this priestly vocation seen for what God intended it to be. But those who are called to live the new life in Christ are also called to this priestly ministry. "And if there are priests in the Church" writes Schmemann, "if there is the priestly vocation in it, it is precisely in order to reveal to each vocation its priestly essence, to make the whole life of all men the liturgy of the Kingdom, to reveal the Church as the Royal Priesthood of the redeemed world."

How does the Christian priest "offer the world to God in a sacrifice of love and praise?" This is done primarily through *intercession* and *offertory*. Christians express their love for "the world" by praying for it, because the world cannot pray for itself. (The prayer, of course, is no substitute for action; it is correlary to the action.)

In the history of the liturgy, intercessory prayer declined as the role of the lay priests in the liturgy declined, because intercessory prayer belongs to the people. In the classical tradition, it was usually the deacon, not the presbyter, who led the intercessions of the faithful. In one form of intercessory prayer, the Bidding Prayer, the deacon announced a bid, and silence was kept before the presiding minister offered the collect so that the faithful could offer their own silent petitions. The collect served to "collect" these petitions, as it were.

After the Reformation, intercessory prayer was restored to evangelical worship, but it was not restored to the people. Vatican II has again incorporated intercession in the Roman

Mass, and the revitalized concept of the general priesthood of believers in the Roman Catholic Church today is evidenced in the fact that many lay people pray petitions and intentions aloud during the general intercessions. Here is one "Catholic" practice that ought to be strongly recommended to our people. And even if the people are not yet ready to pray aloud and spontaneously during the general intercessions, they should be encouraged to present their concerns in written form to the worship leaders so that the intercessions may be specific and all-encompassing.

In the offertory Christians present material gifts which symbolize their self-offering. Today these gifts usually take the form of money, bread and wine. But in earlier times all sorts of material gifts were offered, such as food for the needy. The gifts were brought forward in an offertory procession of the faithful and were collected by the deacons. This liturgical action, restored, would provide a way of enacting the essential Christian sacrifice, "to present your bodies as a living sacrifice, holy and acceptable to God, which is your spiritual worship" (Rom. 12:1).

It is the task of the pastor as worship coordinator to allow the people of God to exercise their priestly ministries. It apparently did not occur to St. Paul that there might be some members of the congregation with no particular task to perform. "To each is given the manifestation of the Spirit for the common good." It also apparently did not occur to St. Paul that one ministerial office in the church would absorb all the other ministerial offices (1 Cor. 12:28). Each of the offices or functions which Paul mentioned in his letters existed not for itself, but for building up of the whole body. There could be no question of rivalry or competition among the members. There are a diversity of gifts, and there is occasion for all of them to be used.

The occasion par excellence for the utilization of the gifts of the members of the congregation is the chief liturgy of the congregation, which brings to focus the whole life and mission of the church. Eugene Brand gives us a vision of how this can work.

> Involvement in the liturgy should be according to the talents and responsibility in the congregation. Hands should do what hands can do, legs what legs can do. It is natural for people with musical talent to be especially active in hymns, anthems, and similar parts of the Service. People gifted in public speaking might read the lessons. People with greater sensitivity to the needs of the congregation and the world at large might share responsibility for the intercessions. Women who bake bread might prepare bread for the sacrament [men too!]: Those who sew could prepare linens and banners. Artists can contribute needful artifacts or design banners and paraments. Young men [and women!] could be of service as ushers or acolytes. Men [and women!] of spiritual maturity might assist the pastor in distributing the bread and wine. With a little applied imagination the list could be extended at will.[2]

It is out of such considerations that worship teams could be developed by the pastor with the help of his worship and music committee. The pastor's role in all this, apart from carrying out the responsibilities of his representative ministry to preach the Word and administer the Sacraments, is to direct and coordinate the involvement of the lay priests in the celebration and performance of the "public work of the people" (which is what *leitourgia* is).

The Development of Worship Teams [3]

The Worship and Music Committee

The Worship and Music Committee is not, properly speaking, one of the worship teams. But it exercises an important function in providing for and leading the worship of the congregation. So its role should be understood.

The Constitutional duties of this committee in many congregations include:

- assisting the church council in seeing that the services are conducted regularly and in accordance with the rites of the Lutheran Church
- recruiting and training competent ushers
- providing and caring for hymnals and other devotional materials
- supervising, and striving to advance the welfare and effective service of, the choirs of the congregation
- arranging for the care of paraments, vestments, and musical instruments and
- in consultation with the pastor, the organist, and the choir director, furnishing appropriate music supplies for use in worship.

This is plenty for the committee to do. But in this day of change in worship materials and practices, there are other requirements which must be made on the parish worship and music committee.

1. It must be on the cutting edge of the congregation. Some of the most creative members of the parish should be members of it. It must display an adventuresome spirit that makes possible both a sensitivity to traditions that are worth preserving and an openness to current developments that are worth implementing.
2. It must study, provide for, and implement new worship materials with an eye toward
   (a) emphasizing creative celebrations
   (b) centering the weekly liturgy on Word and Sacrament
   (c) stirring the congregation to more active involvement in the liturgy
   (d) involving diverse members of the congregation in planning parish liturgies (how about the old people as well as the youth!)
   (e) preparing for the introduction of a new service book and hymnal by the end of this decade and

(f) helping in the formation of worship teams by recommending and equipping members of the congregation to assume leadership roles.

Assisting Ministers

The term "assisting minister" can be used to designate all who exercise leadership roles in the liturgy, such as lectors, cantors, acolytes, and others. Here we are restricting the use of the term to those who function in the traditional diaconal capacity: i.e. to read the Gospel, lead the petitions of the intercessions, and administer the chalice at the communion.

Assisting ministers should be mature Christians, nominated by the pastor, approved by the council, and commissioned or installed to fulfill their responsibilities for a given period of time. In average-sized congregations with one main service each week, six "deacons" would be sufficient. If there are two main services each week, perhaps as many as twelve "deacons" would be needed. This would allow each one to serve two complete months each year. With a larger number of "deacons," there might be a head assisting minister (or "archdeacon"). These persons may or may not be members of the parish council.

These assisting ministers are the *leaders in prayer*. In CW-2 they have the prayer of the day, the petitions in the act of reconciliation and in the intercessions, and the post-communion prayer. There may also be other persons in the congregation who are selected to offer petitions, or there may be spontaneous petitions. These could be offered from the midst of the congregation. However, if the assisting minister is expected to lead the bids and petitions, it may be necessary to have most of them written out. In some standard petitions, blanks can be left where people's names can be inserted (e.g. the leaders of church and state, the hospitalized and ill, those celebrating significant anniversaries, and the faithful departed). It would be good to keep a loose-leaf binder with collections of bids and petitions for various days, seasons, or special events. Exclusive reliance on the prayer formularies provided in such worship helps as *Celebrate* will stifle meaningful, creative, concrete prayer. These insert sheets are helps, not substitutes for the parish's own creativity. They need not be used slavishly: they can be used as springboards to inspire local imaginations.

These assisting ministers are *communion assistants*. They must be taught manual actions and local choreography must be worked out to facilitate the preparation of the gifts, the administration of communion, and clearing the table. In terms of communion practices, the following procedures might be observed:

1. The presiding minister communes himself first, then the assisting minister(s).
2. The presiding minister hands the chalice of wine and a purificator to the assisting minister(s).
3. The assisting minister(s) follow the presiding minister, who administers the bread. This allows the assisting minister(s) to see who is receiving communion and who is not, especially where young children who have not yet received first communion come to the altar rail for a blessing. This also means that the presiding minister must not rush ahead of his assistant(s).
4. The assisting minister uses the purificator to wipe the rim of the chalice after each communicant drinks from it, and turns the chalice before offering it to the next communicant. As he administers the chalice he may say, "The blood of Christ, shed for you."
5. Have an acolyte standing by to refill the chalice when more wine is needed. This prevents the time-consuming necessity of making frequent return trips to the altar.

Lectors

Lectors should be selected from among a wide variety of members of the congregation. There should be a sufficient number of lectors so that they have to read only about one

Sunday every other month. The only requirement is that the lectors be *good readers,* persons who are able to stand before a group of people without getting overly nervous or embarrassed.

Until all the lectors have had experience in reading the lessons, it will be necessary to rehearse them in how to approach the ambo, carry the Bible in the Gospel procession, announce and conclude the readings, and how to read in the particular worship space since acoustics vary from place to place. The pastor need not do this rehearsing if there is somebody in the congregation who has some training in speech or drama. Often high school English teachers have some training in these fields. If they're good at it, they might even be asked to coach the presiding minister in his role.

Acolytes

A question always raised in parishes is: Who should be acolytes? We indicated in Chapter Four that one should avoid using small children. They're cute, but relatively useless as worship leaders. A minimum age might be ten, the age at which many children now receive first communion. There is no maximum age. There is no need to remove a person from acolyte service because of confirmation (first public affirmation of the baptismal covenant), graduation, or marriage. Older youth would probably function best as acolytes.

A number of acolyte organizations throughout the church can provide a model for the parishes. These organizations stress worship education and internal governance which enables older and more experienced acolytes to train and supervise younger and less experienced acolytes. These organizations usually provide for a service of installation, officers, meeting times, training sessions, and service badges (e.g. crosses). Such organizations are especially attractive to young teen-age boys (the same age group as Boy Scouts). An adult member of the worship and music committee might serve as an advisor to the group. And why not have the head acolyte serve as a member of the worship and music committee to help in the planning of services?

In Chapter Four we listed the liturgical roles of the acolyte. Here are additional responsibilities which can be assigned to them.

1. Before the service
   (a) be at church and vested about fifteen minutes before the service starts
   (b) review the service with the pastor to find out if there are any special instructions
   (c) see that the altar area is ready: service books and bulletins in place, altar book and Bible properly marked, candles lighted
   (d) help the pastor and other ministers with vesting if requested
2. During the service
   (a) be attentive and alert and participate in the liturgy
   (b) watch for signals from the pastor
   (c) carry out all assignments in a conspicuous manner
3. After the service
   (a) extinguish the candles during the postlude or after the people have departed
   (b) put the altar area in order: return all books to their proper places, remove all service bulletins, put all furnishings in order
   (c) help the pastor in removing and storing vestments
   (d) store all vestments in their proper closets

Because acolytes have such a conspicuous liturgical role they should be trained:
- how to walk in processions carrying cross, torches, banners, books, etc.
- how to sit with good posture without looking stiff and unatural
- what clues to watch for during the service to let them know when to stand, sit, kneel, receive the offerings, as-

sist with the offerings, assist with the preparation of the vessels at the offertory, receive communion, help clear the table after communion, form processions, etc.

- know how to serve at other services: baptisms, weddings, funerals, vigils, Matins and Vespers, etc.
- know the names of things used in the services, various vessels, linens, furnishings, vestments, etc., so that they can get something when it is needed without a great deal of explanation
- know the order of service and the names of its individual parts so they can act at the proper time. If the pastor says, form the Gospel procession at the beginning of the alleluia verse, or bring the lavabo bowl to the altar at the end of the offertory song, they should know what he is talking about

Ushers

Just as not all people are good public readers, so not all people are good hosts. Ushers should be recruited with some attention to their ability to make worshipers comfortable, to know what material to give to them, to be involved in the action of the service, and to help people exit safely when the service is over. Any member of the parish may serve as an usher, although children should not be used—it just isn't a child's job.

Each parish should have a capable head usher who serves on the worship and music committee, participates in service planning, and is able to supply well-trained ushers when they are needed. The head usher should be appointed for a term of from one to three years, with the possibility of re-appointment. The head usher would appoint assistants, perhaps one for each of the hours when services are held, who would help him recruit other ushers and arrange the usher schedule. Training sessions for ushers should cover the following details.

1. Before the service:
   (a) when to arrive and how soon to be ready for duty
   (b) what "dress code" to observe
   (c) what physical arrangements to be responsible for: setting thermostats, opening windows, turning on lights, unlocking doors, turning on the p.a. system, posting hymn numbers, folding bulletins, setting up extra chairs, etc.
   (d) where to stand to greet the worshipers
   (e) how to keep people out of the rear pews

2. During the service:
   (a) what signals to give to the ministers, acolytes, musicians
   (b) being sensitive to outside distractions and avoid being distractive themselves through unnecessary movement and conversation. The ushers are also worshipers and they should participate in the service along with everyone else.
   (c) what procedures to use for receiving the offering. Marching forward to receive empty plates from the minister is an empty, meaningless gesture. The offering receptacles should be stored at the ushers' station where the ushers can get them when they are needed.
   (d) what procedures to use in presenting the offering. Note that in the Service of the Word (CW-5) there is no need to bring the offering forward to the altar because there is no offertory.
   (e) what procedures to use in ushering people to and from communion without looking like drill sergeants. The practice of continuous communion is preferred to communion by "tables" because it takes less time, eliminates the need to count the number of people for each table, avoids "pressuring" people to go to the altar, and allows people (especially the elderly) to go at their own pace.

3. After the service:
   (a) do not usher people out! Let them leave or stay as they wish. But if they take seriously the dismissal, "Go in peace. Service the Lord," don't get trampled in the stampede
   (b) greet the people as they leave and alert the pastor to visitors
   (c) record attendance figures as may be required
   (d) help to put things in order: i.e. collect used bulletins, close windows, turn off lights, p.a. system, replace service books, lock doors, etc.
   (e) ask if anything else needs to be done before leaving

Musicians and singing groups

By parish musicians we mean those who are hired by the congregation, either full-time or part-time, to give leadership to the parish music program. They would include choir directors and organists, and perhaps also cantors. Whether the parish musicians are full-time or part-time, they must have some necessary credentials to serve a Lutheran congregation.

1. Musicians must know and understand the Lutheran tradition and worship practices. There are plenty of institutes and conferences to which they can be sent for instruction. It's a good idea to see that the parish musicians attend some kind of church music institute at least every other year just so that they can keep abreast of developments in the fields of liturgy and music.

2. Musicians must know how to work with amateur groups and be adept at leading congregational singing. A choir director has to demonstrate tolerance when dealing with largely untrained voices. The fact that an organist is a concert artist is no guarantee that he or she can play or lead with sensitivity congregational singing of hymns and liturgical music.

3. Musicians must be aware of their roles as worship leaders. This is especially true of cantors who function conspic-

uously in the service: but it is no less true of other musicians who function audibly. The parish musicians should be consulted and should help in the planning of services. This means that they should be *ex officio* members of the worship and music committee.

4. Musicians should be "team" people, willing and able to work closely with others in the planning of the service. There's no place here for prima donas. That would violate the corporate character of the church's worship.

5. Musicians should be willing to give leadership to the *whole* musical program of the parish: widening the horizons of the people to encompass various musical forms and techniques, challenging the choirs to rise to the occasion, and encouraging imaginative and creative musical usages in the service. They can be of service to the congregation's education program by providing "music appreciation" courses for the church school, the catechetical classes, and the adult school of religion.

6. Musicians should develop a sense of discernment in the selection of music for the service. Not only should the music itself be of good quality (no matter what *genre* it is), but the texts should reflect sound doctrine and be related to the church year.

Parish choirs

The choirs should consider themselves "worship teams" whose principle task is to lead the congregation in singing hymns and liturgical music. The mere physical presence of the choir usually adds body to congregational singing.

In addition, the choirs should sing music that the congregation is not prepared to sing. This should first of all be liturgical music: psalms at the entrance, after the first lesson, during communion; alleluia verses; parts of canticles (see especially those in CW-5). Preparing an anthem should be a secondary concern. This is not to say that the anthem lacks importance; but it should not be the first order of business.

In fact, it may be asking too much to expect a parish choir to have an anthem prepared for every Sunday and festival. It may make more sense to allow the choirs time to prepare well-done, well-chosen anthems or other special music for festivals of the church year: Advent I, Christmas, Epiphany, Transfiguration, Maundy Thursday, Easter, Pentecost, Reformation, All Saints.

Altar Guilds

The altar guild also forms a "worship team"; in fact, a very important one. Altar guilds have traditionally been women's organizations with auxiliary status in the parish structure. But there is no need to restrict membership to women. Some tasks which an altar guild performs could use male help. And how about the youth?

The responsibilities of the altar guild are so numerous and varied that it's impossible to list them all here. But check lists should be developed that take account of the following areas of responsibility:

- Care of the altar and the altar area
- Care of the liturgical furniture: i.e. ambos, credence table, chairs, etc.
- Care for communion vessels, linens and elements
- Care for baptismal vessels, towels, candles, white garments, oils, etc.
- Care for vestments of pastor, assisting ministers and acolytes
- Preparation for various services during the church year in terms of making or securing special vestments, paraments, banners and decorations
- Preparation for various liturgical acts: Communion, Baptism, Marriage, Funeral, etc., in terms of having ready whatever equipment is needed for the particular rite
- Arrangement of flower schedule and floral displays
- Arrange a schedule of people who will offer the bread and wine for the Eucharist

• Provision for these elements if and when they are not brought and offered by members of the congregation

One thorny question which must be raised here is the disposal of the communion elements after the service. In many parishes the ladies of the altar guild simply put the wafers back in the wrappers and pour the unused wine back in the bottle. What does such a practice suggest about our beliefs concerning the sacrament? Lutherans have never defined the ontological status of the elements after the consecration. This is because Lutherans have not been concerned about a "change" in the elements or the lack of a "change." That has characterized both the Roman Catholic and the Reformed views of the sacrament. If one believes that the bread and wine "change" into the body and blood of Christ at the consecration, then one would not mix the consecrated elements with the unconsecrated. Sacramental reservation would be a logical way to dispose of the elements after the eucharistic celebration. If one believes that the bread and wine are *only* "symbolic reminders" of the body and blood of Christ, the elements can be treated like "mere" bread and wine after the Service. Since neither of these beliefs are compatible with the Lutheran doctrine of the sacrament of the altar, it would seem that neither practice would be totally suitable.

Lutherans have regarded the elements as "visible words." Hence, the elements should be regarded in the same way as words are regarded: as means of communication. The question to be raised, then, is: What are we communicating by what we do? In terms of the disposing of the elements in the light of this criterion, perhaps the best procedure would be to take seriously the meal-character of the sacrament and not have left-overs. The elements should be eaten and consumed, perhaps by all the members of the congregation (a second helping) or at least by the officiating ministers. If, because of the quantity of the elements or other extenuating circumstances, the elements cannot be consumed, then a decision must be made about the disposal. Some of the elements could be reserved if this is a *reservation for use,* i.e. for communion of the sick and shut-in and for use in the next Communion Service. Such a practice would visibly demonstrate the fellowship which exists between the gathered congregation and the absent brethren and the continuity between one service and the next. The bread may be stored in a ciborium and the wine in a small cruet. Excess wine may be poured down a piscina or into the ground. But the practice of returning left-over elements to the supply of unconsecrated elements can only suggest a view of the sacrament which is incompatible with the doctrine of the Real Presence. Luther, in fact, regarded it as a practice "smacking of Zwinglianism." [4] No matter whether a "personal presence" of Christ in the sacrament is emphasized, the Lutheran Confessions still teach a "sacramental union" between the body and blood of Christ and the bread and wine. Here is a classic case, then, where practice informs belief, and vice versa. Working out the details of how to dispose of the elements will provide an opportunity for members of the altar guild to come to grips with what they really believe about the sacrament.

6

Education for Worship

The Pastor as Teacher: Opportunities to Teach

The church receives its identity and cohesion as the new people of God in the act of worship. Where the Word is rightly proclaimed and where the Sacraments are rightly administered, there is the church (AC VII)—"rightly" being understood as according to the divine institution and purpose. It has been the purpose of God's Word throughout salvation history to call together a people who shall be God's own; the Sacraments have served to form that people into a holy community. Because this takes place in the worship event the pastor will want to see that continuing education opportunities are provided for his people in this activity.

Opportunities for worship education present themselves in catechetical classes, adult forums, inquirers' sessions, and in preaching. The introduction and texts of the ILCW's *Contemporary Worship* booklets can be used in adult classes as the basis for discussion. A book like Eugene Brand's *The Rite Thing* provides a fine six-week course in liturgical renewal. Poets, musicians, and artists can be brought into a class session to relate how they express their faith through the art-forms of the twentieth century.

In recent years there has been a growing lack of confidence in what can be accomplished through preaching. We have stressed doing more than saying in this book. It is a pedagogical insight that people learn more from doing than from merely hearing. But this in no way denies that the spoken word can be a source of power when it concretely touches people's lives. Our concern with preaching under the heading of worship education is to point out that the liturgy itself provides concrete sermon "illustrations." If the sermon alludes to liturgical acts and texts the congregation can more easily see the connection of the liturgy with the Gospel. Moreover, the Sacraments are concrete forms of Gospel-proclamation. As divinely-instituted means of grace, preaching cannot refrain from pointing to them as especially promised ways in which the grace of God comes into people's lives.

It should also be remembered that preaching is a liturgical act. It has its setting in the liturgy, and it should reflect the style and content of the rest of the liturgy. Sometimes in the past the liturgy had to bear the Gospel alone when preaching degenerated into moralism. Moralism is no less a temptation for preachers today. When this temptation strikes the preacher has recourse to the hermeneutic provided by the liturgy itself. It is, from start to finish, a proclamation and celebration of the mighty acts of God in Christ. That is also the content of evangelical preaching. The preacher should always ask himself: does my sermon proclaim and celebrate what God has done, what he is capable of doing now, and what he will surely do again? Is the gift of grace conveyed by my sermon, or only the demands of the Law?

There are other opportunities for worship education in the parish which should not be missed. Chief among these are *training sessions for ushers and acolytes.* Both groups need to know the shape and content of the liturgies of the church: Holy Communion, the Service of the Word, Matins and Vespers, and Marriage and Funeral Services. Ushers and acolytes serve at these services and they need to know and understand what is happening so that their service is more sensitive. In addition, acolytes will need to know the names and uses of vestments, vessels, and furnishings if their assistance is going to be really helpful. Instruction on these things should be provided at training sessions. Moreover, the pastor should not underestimate the natural curiosity and desire to learn on the part of adolescent acolytes. It's not unusual for acolytes to consider the possibility of future ordination as a result of their service experience. The pastor should not push this, but it is symptomatic of their growing desire to be directly involved in the life of the church.

At the beginning of the fall activity season, when the choir begins to assemble once again for regular rehearsals, the pastor should make a point of attending the first few meetings to give the choir pep talks about their role as worship leaders. He might also relate to them something about new worship materials being provided by the church bodies, especially if he wants to introduce these materials to congregational use. It is a common suggestion today on the part of church planners that new ideas should be widely owned and not be just imposed by the pastor.

Another group which should share ownership of new ideas is the altar guild. The work of the guild creates a curiosity about liturgical matters. This curiosity should be both satiated and widened through ongoing study and discussion. The pastor should want to assist the guild in its study program by suggesting resources and by being willing to attend guild meetings on occasion to share new ideas.

Finally, there are at least two *counseling situations* which provide the pastor with an opportunity for worship education: pre-baptismal and pre-marital instruction. The thrust of baptismal instruction with candidates and/or sponsors is the new life into which one is initiated in Holy Baptism. This new life in Christ is rooted in the sacramental economy of salvation. The content of baptismal instruction, therefore, allows easy reference to the liturgies of Holy Baptism and Holy Communion. These liturgies may serve as the starting point for instruction on the new life in Christ because they ritualize a reality which is already taking place in the lives of the persons involved and in the life of the community into which the candidates are about to be assimilated.

A similar use can be made of the Marriage Service in premarital counseling. It provides a convenient way of understanding the meaning of Christian marriage. It also ritualizes what should be happening between the bride and groom— growth and fidelity and love. If the marriage is celebrated in the context of the eucharistic meal, the pastor has an opportunity to discuss the nature and benefits of Holy Communion and to show how Christ becomes the third partner in Christian marriage, present to strengthen the bonds between the other two partners.

Introducing Liturgical Change

The various opportunities for worship education which are available to the pastor will have to be fully exploited in this time of drastic, and sometimes even radical, change in worship habits. News of the production of a new worship book and hymnal has sparked a great deal of agitation and apprehension in congregations because, in fact, the people *do own* their own liturgies and hymns and they will not readily or willingly surrender these to liturgical commissions to be changed by authoritarian fiat. This has been the case no less in Roman Catholic congregations than in Lutheran and other Protestant congregations.

In defense of liturgical commissions, it must be said that they have proceeded with far more grass roots experimentation and evaluation than has previously been the case. The sheer number of people who have been involved in the work of the Inter-Lutheran Commission on Worship, is staggering. Here is no case of "experts" telling pastors and congregations what to do! But at some point decisions must finally be made and a new book published. In expectation of new materials being authorized by the churches, pastors can involve their people in what we might call "change therapy."

A starting point in "change therapy" is getting people to recognize that *change is a way of life*. Societies and individuals may resist change; but they will either change or die. Change in the world around us impinges on us. We are affected by changes in our neighborhoods, our places of work, our job description, our family patterns, and in our churches. Changes in national and international politics, economics, merchandising, transportation, communication, education, medicine, etc., effect our lives and *change us*. We are not the same persons we once were. In an age of "future shock" we are even surprised if we can keep up with the changes around us.

These kinds of changes should be discussed in adult forums. Taking note of them will provide neither comfort nor an answer to the question, "why can't we do things the way we always have?" But there is also theological input in this discussion of change. Change occurs in the church because, whatever else the church is, it is a people for whom change is a way of life. *Conversion,* which is personal change and transformation, is the basis of baptismal living, putting to death the old self so that the new self may arise daily to live before God forever. Each day there should be the possibility of cleansing, growth and insight created by a Spirit who pulls and pushes us toward the future fulfillment of all things in God's kingdom.

If people were honest with themselves, they would most likely admit that "the way things were" was not so good. Things may not be satisfying now, either, but this only points out that people long for fulfillment of one type or another. Christians live by hope, awaiting delivery on the promised fulfillment in the future of God. They cannot be satisfied with what is because they await something better. This was well put in a sermon delivered by John Donne in 1627 when he said: "Creatures of an inferiour nature are possest with the *present; Man* is a future *Creature*." [1] Christian man is especially a future creature. He is a pilgrim who has here "no

abiding city." He is always on the move, pressing onward toward the horizon of promise, kept on his restless journey by
the vision of what may yet be. This Abrahamic spirituality is
the very life-blood of Protestantism. It is a spirituality which
is even able to argue with God, because he has been known
on occasion to change his mind and "repent" of what he intended to do.

But even if God and his will do not change, our perception
of his will for us does. If it didn't, there would be no possibility of conversion, and no new insight. As our perception
of God's will for us changes, so does our worship. We try to
find forms which can measure up to the celebration of our
new life in Christ. We try to find language which says more
precisely what we want to say to God in prayer and to one
another in proclamation. We encourage our contemporaries
to express their faith in their own idioms of art and music.
We also rummage through the warehouse of the Christian
tradition to find forms and practices that might be more
"relevant" to our needs today than the ones we are presently
using. Part of being "catholic," as G. K. Chesterton used to
say, is being able to bring one age to the rescue of another.

Changes in worship, therefore, do not occur in a vacuum.
They are directly related to the life of faith. They occur when
Christians experience the grace of God in new ways and try
to find appropriate expressions of prayer, praise and thanksgiving by which to respond to God's grace in their lives and
in their world.

Changes in liturgy also reflect changes in our culture because cult and culture stand in a most dependent relationship
to each other. Christians are not disembodied spirits; they live
in "this world" and they must use the means available in this
world as vehicles for their worship. Our worship may be
joined with that of "the angels and archangels and the whole
company of heaven," but it is still the worship of earthly
creatures and at its best it partakes of an earthly character.

At this point we must enter a disclaimer. Change for the

sake of change is no great advance; nor may change always lead to a positive outcome. Very often the conservatives of the world have been right (no pun intended). The biblical prophets were always reminding Israel of the "good old days" in the wilderness when the people lived by grace alone. Reformers in the history of the church have always appealed to the "good old days" of primitive Christianity when discipleship and faith counted for something. The sixteenth century Reformation itself was radical because it proposed a "return to the sources" of Scripture and the Fathers. Reformers of liturgy have also hankered for some "golden age" in the past, whether their idea of that "golden age of worship" was the sixteenth century, the thirteenth, the fourth, or the first.[2]

On the other hand, to cling to the forms of the past or to particular worship books as though they were good for all time exemplifies a spirit of legalism which is incompatible with both evangelical freedom and tradition in the true sense of the term. For tradition is not something fixed in the past in all details, never to be changed. It is a pattern passed on in its essentials from one living community to another, but always being adapted in its particulars to the contemporary community.[3]

Lutheran liturgical practice has been characterized by evangelical freedom. The proliferation of church orders in the sixteenth and seventeenth centuries witnesses to this. Martin Luther himself advised his followers to maintain a flexibility of usage when he wrote concerning his own *German Mass,* "This or any other order shall be so used that whenever it becomes an abuse, it shall straightway be abolished and replaced by another." [4] While Lutherans have been concerned to preserve what is essential in Christian worship, they have demonstrated a remarkable flexibility in the use of outward forms such as language and music, rites and ceremonies. The Augsburg Confession witnesses to the early Lutheran practice of adding German songs here and there in the Mass among the parts sung in Latin (AC XXIV). Actually, any service could be celebrated completely in German or in Latin. A German song could be substituted for any Latin chant. Or, to any Latin chant a German song could be added. Since the German songs were derived largely from a folk idiom, this might suggest possibilities for the blending of contemporary-folk and traditional linguistic and musical elements in the service.

Even more remarkable is the openness and responsiveness of Lutheran musicians to the musical culture and environment of their times. This meant, in the Baroque period, for example, that Italian madrigal and operatic styles found their way into the compositions of North German church composers, producing the artistry of a Michael Praetorius, a Heinrich Schütz, and a J. S. Bach. The same kind of openness to culture and environment characterizes the work of such notable contemporary church composers as Hugo Distler, H. F. Micheelsen, Ernst Pepping, Jan Bender, and Heinz Werner Zimmerman.[5] Zimmerman, for example, juxtaposes elements of jazz with the polyphonic motet. Through organ pieces, choral works, and a few new hymn tunes, the sounds of the twentieth century can be heard in our churches, and they might affect what we think we're doing in the place of worship.

The forms and expressions of Christian worship have varied with changes in culture from Semitic to Greek, from Greek to Latin, from Latin to German, from German to American; and now changes are again taking place in the forms and expressions of worship as the liturgy moves from a base in Western culture to a base in African and Asian cultures. But in all of this change from one culture to another the *essence* of Christian worship remains unchanged. The essential heart of Christian worship is the proclamation of the Word and the celebration of the sacraments. We still do today what Christians of the first generation did when "they devoted themselves to the apostles' teaching and fellowship, to the breaking of bread and the prayers" (Acts 2:42). It may be useful in parish study groups to isolate the elements which are at the center of the liturgy from those which are at its circumference.[6]

The Center of the Liturgy

There are those who think that the worship of the early church was bare and simple. To be sure, it was not as elaborate and as splendid as solemn high mass in the Notre Dame Cathedral. But Christian liturgy did not come into being *ex nihilo*. The Liturgy of the Word evolved from the Jewish Synagogue Service. The Liturgy of the Eucharistic Meal evolved from the Jewish Passover Seder (or some other type of Jewish sacred meal). When the Jewish forms passed over into Christian usage they were filled with new content. Jesus gave a new interpretation to the Scripture readings when he preached in the Synagogues: the Scriptures were fulfilled in Jesus himself. When he instituted his own meal in the Upper Room it signified the new covenant between God and humanity which was ratified by Jesus' own sacrifice on the cross.

The Liturgy of the Word comprises, as a minimum, readings from Holy Scripture. These readings have been traditionally selected from the Old Testament, the apostolic writings in the New Testament, and the four Gospels. It is thought that the lectionary system developed in the church from the attempt to correlate the reading of the apostolic writings and the Gospels with the already established sequence of readings from the *Torah* and *Haftorah* in the Synagogue.[7]

These readings were interspersed with the singing of psalms which varied the pace of the liturgy and provided prayerful reflection on the readings. Preaching was added to expound the meaning of the Scriptures and to apply them to daily life. The Christian Liturgy of the Word included intercessory prayer for all sorts and conditions of people. The model for this may have been the great intercessory prayer of the Synagogue, called *tefillah* ("the prayer"), the so-called Eighteen Benedictions.

The Liturgy of the Eucharistic Meal comprises, as a minimum, the presentation of the bread and wine on the table, the consecration of these gifts by a great Prayer of Thanksgiving, the breaking of the bread, and the distribution of both elements. Gregory Dix has popularized what has come to be called "the four-action shape of the liturgy." While this may be a historical oversimplification, the catechetical usefulness of the "four-action shape" cannot be denied. According to the narratives of the institution of the Lord's Supper in the New Testament, our Lord did *take* the bread and wine, *give thanks* over them, *break* the bread, and *give* the elements to his disciples. If the bread and wine are treated separately, seven actions are involved. But at some point early in the history of the liturgy, probably at the point where the Lord's Supper was separated from the Agape meal, the bread and wine were treated together. From this fusion of the actions concerning the two elements Gregory Dix postulated the evolution of the Offertory, the Eucharistic Prayer, the Fraction, and the Distribution.[8] To these liturgical acts were added the Lord's Prayer before the Communion, a Post-Communion Prayer, and a Benediction and Dismissal.

We cannot just pass over the controversy which has erupted in some Lutheran circles regarding the application of this "four-action shape" in the ILCW *Service of Holy Communion* (CW-2). The most persistent critic of this "shape" has objected to the implication that it obligates the use of the fraction ceremony.[9] The Lutheran reformers rightly objected to all the allegorical symbolism which became attached to the fraction during the Middle Ages. They also objected to Zwingli's insistence on the use of such ceremonial actions as the fraction to summon up an affective remembrance of Jesus' meals with his disciples. The Calvinists regarded the fraction as a necessary ceremony in the Lord's Supper because Jesus did it in the Upper Room. In fact, it became a mark of profession of faith among them just as the elevation did among the Lutherans. But the Lutheran Confessions also assert that

"the entire action of the Lord's Supper as Christ ordained it"
is to be observed.

> But the command of Christ, "Do this," which compre-
> hends the whole action or administration of this sacra-
> ment (namely, that in a Christian assembly we take bread
> and wine, consecrate it, distribute it, receive it, eat and
> drink it, and therewith proclaim the Lord's death), must
> be kept integrally and inviolately, just as St. Paul sets the
> whole action of the breaking of bread, or of the distri-
> bution and reception, before our eyes in 1 Cor. 10:16.[10]

The use of whole loaves will once again necessitate the breaking of bread, at least as a utilitarian act. But it cannot be a
"mere" utilitarian act, any more than the administration of
the wine from a common cup can be. Someone is sure to
notice the same thing St. Paul did: "Because there is one loaf,
we who are many are one body, for we all partake of the
same loaf" (1 Cor. 10:17). The fraction demonstrates the
unity of the many in the one, and thereby connects the church
and the sacrament.

The Circumference of the Liturgy

When Christians moved into larger buildings it was necessary to adapt the style of worship to the new settings. The
kind of liturgy that could be celebrated in a private house
or a small building would not work in a great basilica. For
one thing, it took time to get the ministers to their places
in the church. To "cover" their entrance and make the beginning of the liturgy more solemn, music was added: the
Introit or entrance psalm sung by the choir; the *Kyrie*, a peti-
tionary prayer in litany form sung by the deacon and the
people; and the *Gloria in excelsis* sung as the "opening hymn."
By the time this singing was finished the ministers were in
their places in the apse and the bishop could greet the people
and offer a short prayer for the day (the Collect).

Because of the larger congregations it took more time to

gather the gifts of the people and to distribute the sacramental elements. So "cover music" was added at these places
also: the offertory and communion anthems, which were
originally psalms or parts of psalms. By the time of the Reformation hymns were also sung during the distribution.

In the Middle Ages the priest and his assistants said prayers
of preparation in the sacristy before the beginning of the
Mass. This is the origin of the *Confiteor* or Confession of Sins.
These prayers were at first eliminated by the reformers. But
devotional attachment to them prompted the reformers later
on to revise them into a preparatory act for the whole congregation. With the demise of private confession, in spite of
all the reformers could do to retain it, the Confession of Sins
at the beginning of the liturgy took on a more important function.

Finally, hymns were added to the liturgy during and after
the Reformation to encourage and facilitate congregational
participation. Thus, over the centuries the beginning of the
liturgy was greatly expanded. Today all of this "entrance"
material is still used even though most of it no longer "covers"
an actual entrance. Pruning down the beginning of the liturgy
has proven very difficult, however, because of devotional attachment to these prayers and canticles.

This kind of historical review should have a liberating effect
with regard to liturgical change. It should help people to
understand what is essential to the Liturgy and what can be
added or subtracted as necessity requires. But when all is said
and done, pastors still must exercise care for the "weaker
brethren." Lutheranism from the beginning was unwilling to
put people into "bad faith" through reckless change. In some
ways that turned out to be beneficial because it preserved
some things for the Lutheran cultus which might otherwise
have gotten lost in an iconoclastic shuffle. But at the same
time, it must be asserted that change should not be seen as
a threat to Christians; it is a promise: "Behold, I make all
things new." That promise of Christ must be proclaimed in

uncompromising ways. Zeal for the fulfillment of that promise should itself adjust people to change. But if that doesn't happen, we will have to turn to strategies and techniques of implementation.

Strategies for Change

The pastor should first introduce new worship material to the worship and music committee, ask them how they envision this material being used in the congregation, and then get them to bring a resolution to the church council that the material be tested for a period of weeks with the understanding that the congregation will be given instruction before it is used and will be given an opportunity to react to and evaluate the material at the end of the period of experimental use.

In preparation for the actual use of the material by the congregation, the choir should set aside rehearsal time to learn whatever new music there might be in this material. Members of the congregation, and particularly the council and the worship and music committee, should be invited to attend these rehearsals so that a larger group of people will be familiar with the material when it is actually used. At the rehearsal the pastor should explain the rationale for the new material. A congregational sing-a-long will be especially helpful when the new hymnal is ready for use.

If it is a new service which is being introduced, copies of it should be in the pews for a month. During this time the people can be asked to follow the new service and join in the spoken responses. The choir will sing all the musical parts. After each use of the service during that month the pastor can explain parts of it to the congregation and the choir director can rehearse some of the music with the congregation. This seems to work better than rehearsing and explaining before the service starts. Such a procedure can be threatening. It is better to let the people experience the service before it is discussed. Having already been exposd to it they might find that they actually like it.

Finally, after the period of full, actual use the people should be given an opportunity to react to and evaluate the service. If questionnaires are used the people should be informed of the results. The worship leaders of the denomination should know the results too if the material is authorized for provisional use. As far as possible, a liturgy must belong to the people if it is to serve as an effective vehicle of their "public work." The belief-structures and behavioral patterns of a community must be capable of being expressed through the liturgy.

Calendar Possibilities

One of the best ways of providing for ongoing worship education in the parish is through a creative following of the church year. The liturgical movement has seen the church year as a means of progressively unfolding the mystery of redemption in Christ and as a way of forming the faithful into a pattern of Christian life.

The reform of the church year in CW-6: *The Church Year Calendar and Lectionary* represents an effort at pruning and simplifying the calendar which has been shared by a number of Western churches. The revised calendar centers on the two pivotal events of salvation-history: the incarnation and the passion/resurrection of Jesus Christ. Each of these events is celebrated during a season which focuses entirely on it: Christmas-Epiphany and Easter. Each of these seasons is preceded by a time of preparation: Advent and Lent. That's all there is to the festival times of the church year. The so-called "green Sundays" are ordinary, with no specific seasonal content. During the Sundays after Epiphany and Pentecost (except for the Sundays immediately following, which are, respectively, the Baptism of our Lord and the Festival of the Holy Trinity) the readings generally follow a *lectio continua* pattern, although there is usually some correlation between the First Lesson and the Gospel on these days.

In addition to the "temporal cycle" of festivals, the church has a "sanctoral cycle." The new church year calendar in CW-6 provides a multitude of commemorations of heroes of the faith: martyrs, apostles, pastors, teachers, reformers, etc. The commemoration of martyrs constitutes one of the oldest types of celebrations in Christian history. Except for the capital letter days of biblical saints, it is not expected that congregations will observe *all* of the commemorations suggested in CW-6. Rather, congregations would select from the list those commemorations which are especially meaningful to the local community of faith. Often there is an ethnic identification. Sometimes a commemoration is meaningful because it corresponds with the way in which a particular congregation perceives its life and work. These commemorations should be viewed as extensions of Christ's incarnation and passion-resurrection. Thus, they provide concrete examples in history of the church's central affirmation and celebration. The example and power of Christ's life and work are seen in the lives and works of the saints, just as it should be seen in our life and work. Commemorations of the saints, therefore, are ultimately a remembrance of Christ himself, especially the mystery of his passion and triumph.

Liturgical Colors

CW-6 urges a greater exploitation of the resources of liturgical colors to bring out the meanings of particular days and seasons than has been the case in the immediate past. To white, red, purple, green, and black—which suggest, respectively, purity, passion, royalty, growth, and death—CW-6 adds gold, the color of solemnity, and blue, the color of hope. Thus, the following scheme is presented for the use of liturgical colors during the church year.

Advent season—blue or purple
Christmas Eve—gold or white
Christmas season through the Baptism of our Lord—white

Sundays after the Epiphany—green
Transfiguration (end of Epiphany season)—white
Ash Wednesday—black or purple
Lent—earthen colors (tan-brown) or purple
Palm Sunday—red or purple
Maundy Thursday—white or purple or red
Good Friday—red or black
Easter Day—gold or white
Easter season—white
Pentecost—red
Trinity Sunday—white
Sundays after Pentecost—green
Christ the King (end of Pentecost season)—white

Blue is suggested for use in Advent as an alternative to purple because it is the color of hope and it therefore highlights the eschatological expectation which characterizes this season. Gold is suggested for use on Christmas and Easter to highlight the solemnity of these two pivotal days in the church year. Black is suggested for Ash Wednesday because this is the most sombre day of the year. It is like a Christian *Yom Kippur,* a day of humiliation and repentance. The back color suggests the ashes to which everything mortal eventually turns. Earthen colors or unbleached linens might be used from Ash Wednesday to the Saturday before the Sunday of the Passion (Palm Sunday). This is an old English custom which suggests the austerity of the Lenten discipline of almsgiving, prayer, and fasting. Dark red is suggested as a color for Holy Week to indicate the intensity of our Lord's passion. It should be a deeper shade of red than that used for Pentecost and festivals of the church.

The usual colors for the lesser festivals are red and white. Red is the color for all commemorations of martyrs and festivals of the church. The darker red of the passion might be used on martyr's days and the brighter red of Pentecost might be used for church festivals. White is the color for all festivals of our Lord, e.g. The Name of Jesus, The Presentation, The Annunciation, The Visitation; and saints' days on which the theme of martyrdom is not present, e.g. St. John, The Confession of St. Peter, The Conversion of St. Paul, The Nativity of St. John the Baptist, St. Mary Magdalen, Mary the Mother of our Lord, and All Saints' Day. Special commemorations for Christian unity, a harvest festival, or a national holiday use the color of the season. The color of vestments and paraments used at weddings and funerals might either be white or the color of the day or season.

Customs and Special Liturgies

It is in the observance of special customs and liturgies that the church year can be utilized to its best advantage as a means of forming the faithful into a pattern of Christian life. There are many local and ethnic customs which can be exploited to good advantage in some parishes. The following suggestions, however, are based on the mainstream of Christian practice and are deeply rooted in the liturgical tradition.

Advent. The most common special custom of Advent is the lighting of the Advent wreath during the responsorial psalm to symbolize the light of vigilance which is kept burning in expectation of the coming of the Bridegroom. Expectation is not fulfillment; nor is coming the same as arrival. This means that Christmas themes should not intrude on Advent. Even the *Gloria in excelsis* should be suppressed during these four weeks of preparation. This will help intensify the feeling of anticipation, especially as the time of Christmas draws nearer.

Christmas. The traditional times of Christmas services are midnight on Christmas Eve, and dawn and mid-morning on Christmas Day. Propers are provided for all three of these occasions. Parishes should at least provide different services for Christmas Eve and Christmas Day. The theme of the Christmas Eve service is the historical nativity of the Christ.

The theme of the Christmas Day service is the meaning of the Incarnation. The Eucharist should be celebrated both days, for these are completely different services.

A special feature of the Christmas Eve service might be a visit to the manger at the end of the service. All the children present in the congregation can be invited to cluster around the manger scene and kneel before the Christ child. It would be an appropriate time to sing some cradle hymn like "Away in a Manger." The Benediction could be given from the manger scene after the cradle hymn.

Candlelight is popular in congregations on Christmas Eve, a reminder of the fact that this was once a Vigil Service. If the candles held by the people in their hands are to be lighted at some time during the service, it ought to be at that point where Christ the Light of the World has come and is really present among his own. This would be at the Communion. As the people receive the sacramental elements an acolyte can follow the ministers and light the hand-held candles with a taper. By the end of the Communion everyone's candle will be lighted and it would be an appropriate time to sing the *Nunc dimittis*.

Epiphany. The Epiphany Gospel, the visit of the Magi, can be liturgically dramatized at the Offertory with the presentation of gifts of gold, frankincense and myrrh, along with other gifts from the people. Epiphany would be a time for using incense in the service and for forming an offertory procession of the people. One old Epiphany custom is the burning of the greens on the "twelfth night." This would appropriately be done outside the church building after the service. Some congregations have developed the custom of saving the trunk of the Christmas tree to make a cross out of it during Lent. This helps to establish the relationship between the crib and the cross, to underscore the idea that the Christ was born to die a sacrificial death.

Ash Wednesday. The name of the day derives from the action of applying ashes on the foreheads of the people in the sign of the cross. It is an outward indication of their inner resolve to mortify the flesh, "ashes to ashes, dust to dust." CW-6, p. 67, makes provision for the restoration of this custom in Lutheran churches. After the sermon those who wish to receive ashes come forward to the communion rail. As the minister makes the sign of the cross on the foreheads of the people, he says, "Remember, O man, that you are dust, and to dust you shall return."

An invitation to the Lenten Discipline of almsgiving, prayer, and fasting (the three notable duties in Matthew 6) should be given either as a part of the Sermon or after it. A Litany of Repentance might take the place of the general intercessions on this day. Such a litany is provided in the Episcopalian *Prayer Book Studies* 19, pp. 162 ff.

Lent. The Gospel on the First Sunday in Lent is the story of the temptations of Jesus in the wilderness. We are reminded that Lent is a time of struggle in a wilderness, a wilderness being a place or a situation in which familiar landmarks and customary supports have disappeared. Liturgical changes in the service during Lent will help to intensify the feeling of being in a spiritual wilderness and of the need to return to the basics of the faith. The liturgical music used during Lent is usually different than that used during the rest of the church year. The *Gloria in excelsis* and the Alleluias are suppressed. Parishes which celebrate the Eucharist every Sunday might replace the Nicene Creed with the Apostles', since the latter is the baptismal profession of faith.

Lent is a time to return, as it were, to the catechumenate. The season originally functioned as a time when the catechumens were prepared for their baptism at the Easter Vigil. Candidates for baptism were declared elect, or *competentes,* at the beginning of Lent. During the third, fourth, and fifth weeks of Lent the Four Gospels, the Creed, and the Lord's

Prayer were "handed over" to them (the *traditio*). This was done publicly so that the faithful overheard the catechetical instruction given to the candidates.[11] In this way the congregation was put in mind of its own need for ongoing conversion and transformation in Christ. This was also a way for the whole congregation to return to the basics of the faith each year, to return to the catechumenate. These ancient practices might once again be relevant to a church in a missionary situation, such as in the urban scene, where the baptism of adults occurs more frequently than the baptism of young children. Even where this is not the case, it would prove profitable to rehearse with the congregation what the Catechism teaches concerning the Ten Commandments, the Apostles' Creed, and the Lord's Prayer on the third, fourth, and fifth Sundays in Lent.

The theme of the Passion is also central to the season of Lent. If a large wooden cross is erected in the church building during this season, something should be done with it to let it remind the congregation of the call to and the costs of discipleship—following the way of the cross. At the end of the service the ministers might proceed to the place of the cross and kneel before it while the congregation sings a hymn of veneration of the cross, such as "Sing, my tongue, the glorious battle," "Sweet the moments, rich in blessing, Which before the cross we spend," "In the Cross of Christ I glory," "Print thine image pure and holy on my heart, O Lord of grace," "The royal banners forward go," or "When I survey the wondrous Cross."

Palm Sunday. The blessing of palms and the procession into the church building mark the beginning of this service. An order for the blessing of palms and the procession is provided in CW-6, p. 74. We suggested in chapter four that the procession include the whole congregation, and that it should begin outside the church building.

The Gospel of the Triumphal Entry of Christ into Jerusalem

is read during the rite of blessing at the beginning of the service. The Gospel during the service is the Passion of our Lord from St. Matthew, St. Mark, and St. Luke in their respective years during the three year cycle of readings. It is from the reading of the passion narrative that this Sunday received its name, the Sunday of the Passion. The most effective way to read the Passion is to have several readers, each taking the parts of various persons: the Evangelist, Jesus, Pilate, the disciples, etc. If copies of the Passion are distributed, the congregation can read the lines of the crowd. In this way everyone is involved in the Passion. We were there, and it is also contemporaneous with us. The great Lutheran composers of the Baroque period accomplished this kind of anamnesic or memorial situation by interspersing verses from the passion narrative with stanzas from the passion chorales. This could still be done, although it might make the service a bit long for contemporary stamina.

Maundy Thursday. There are more special historic rites for Maundy Thursday than for any other day in the church year. One obvious one, from which the day receives its name, is the *Mandatum,* or Footwashing Ceremony. This takes place after the sermon. Persons representing various age groups in the congregation, twelve in number, could be selected to have their feet washed by the pastor. During the footwashing the choir and congregation read antiphonally the verses from John 13 which relate to the institution and meaning of this ceremony.

The *act of reconciliation* should be very meaningful on this day which, in the ancient church, was the day of the reconciliation of the public penitents. In our spiritualized modern practice we have all become penitents during Lent. But the kiss of peace should be genuine and robust on this night. In his *Formula Missae,* Luther regarded the greeting of peace as "a public absolution of the sins of the communicants, the true voice of the gospel announcing remission of sins, and therefore the one and most worthy preparation for the Lord's Table. . . ." [12] If the Service of Public Confession is held on a previous day during Holy Week, the confession of sins might be suppressed on Maundy Thursday to emphasize the joy of reconciliation with God and with one another which is manifested at the Lord's Supper.

Maundy Thursday is the anniversary of the institution of the Lord's Supper. On this day it is fitting that those to whom the ministry of Christ's Word and Sacraments was committed in ordination join together in *concelebration*. Ordained ministers who are present might be vested and surround the presiding minister at the altar during the Eucharistic Prayer. The presiding minister should be the "senior" of the ministerium in that place. The concelebrating clergy need not recite the Words of Institution in unison or break up the Eucharistic Prayer into sections, as is usually done; but they should all participate in the distribution.

After the communion and the post-communion prayer, the choir and congregation may sing or say Psalm 22 antiphonally while the ministers and acolytes *strip the altar* of all vessels, books, and paraments. This action evokes the humiliation of Christ, which is reinforced with the recitation of the passion psalm. When everything has been removed the ministers, choir, and people leave quietly. No benediction is given because the Maundy Thursday Service is only the beginning of the *Triduum of the Passion*. The span of time between Maunday Thursday and Holy Saturday constitutes one continuous liturgy which comes to an end only with the conclusion of the Easter Vigil. The altar and chancel area may be left bare for Good Friday.

Good Friday is an a-liturgical day. That means the Eucharist is not celebrated on it, Lutheran practice notwithstanding. It may be that some people desire to receive the sacrament on Good Friday. This desire can be met by setting aside the elements from the Maundy Thursday celebration. Since the liturgy actually continues on Good Friday even those who are strict about the *extra usus* doctrine need not be alarmed. When all have communed on Maundy Thursday, the remaining elements are carried in procession to an "altar of repose," which might be set up in a chapel. The "altar of repose" should be arrayed in white and banked with flowers. During the procession a suitable sacramental hymn, such as *Adoro te, devote* (SBH #272) may be sung. Members of the congregation can be invited to remain after the service to keep vigil before the reserved sacrament, the presence of Christ for us, just as the disciples were asked to keep watch in the garden of Gethsemane on the night of our Lord's betrayal and arrest.

Good Friday. The ancient liturgy of Good Friday is a form of the Liturgy of the Word before excessive expansion took place in the entrance rite. It is one of the most primitive liturgies to survive from the early church. It is a clear case of the operation of Baumstark's Law: "Primitive conditions are maintained with greater tenacity in the more sacred seasons of the Liturgical Year." [13] A form of the Good Friday liturgy is provided in *Holy Week and Easter: Liturgical Orders Supplementing the Service Book and Hymnal.* We give below a fuller form of it which includes the Gallican additions of the Reproaches and the Veneration of the Cross. For these texts see the *New Roman Sacramentary.*

> The altar should be completely bare, without cloths, candles, or cross.
>
> The ministers go to the altar silently, kneel or prostate themselves, and pray silently for a while.
>
> The Prayer of the Day (without salutation or greeting)
>
> The First Lesson: Isaiah 52:13-53:12
>
> Psalm 22; antiphon: verse la
>
> The Second Lesson: Hebrews 4:14-5:10
>
> The Gradual Verse
>
> The Passion according to St. John (read the same way as the Passion on Palm Sunday)

A Hymn and a Homily may follow.
The Bidding Prayer (SBH, p. 236)
The Veneration of the Cross

The rite of the veneration of the cross may be conducted in this way. The ministers go to the back of the church where the large wooden cross used during Lent has been placed. The presiding minister sings, "This is the wood of the cross, on which hung the Savior of the world." The people respond, "Come, let us worship." The cross is carried by assistants, accompanied by two acolytes with lighted candles. In the middle of the church and again at the chancel the procession stops and the invitatory is sung. While the cross is erected in front of the altar with the two torches on either side of it, two lectors or cantors read or sing the Reproaches. At the end of the Reproaches, all kneeling, the cantor sings one of the profoundest of all liturgical antiphons: "We venerate your cross, O Christ, and praise and glorify your holy resurrection; for by the cross joy has come to the whole world." Then Psalm 67:2 is sung: "God be gracious and bless us; and let his face shed its light upon us." The antiphon is repeated. The congregation joins in singing the veneration hymn, "Sing, my tongue, the glorious battle" (SBH # 61; WS # 728).

Those who desire to receive communion remain. The altar is covered with a cloth and corporal and the sacrament is brought to it without a procession from the altar of repose. The Order of the Communion is as follows:

The Lord's Prayer
The Agnus Dei
The Communion
A Post-Communion Prayer

The people should be informed that this is the pre-sanctified sacrament. It has already been consecrated and set aside. Again, no benediction is given at the end of the Good Friday liturgy. The people should depart silently.

The Office of Tenebrae is becoming popular in Lutheran parishes. Offices of Tenebrae are provided for Thursday, Friday and Saturday in Holy Week in *Holy Week and Easter: Liturgical Orders Supplementing the Service Book and Hymnal.*

Tenebrae is a special form of the Divine Office for Holy Week. Originally it was a kind of vigil held in the early morning. But for centuries now the hour of observance has been moved up so that the Office is recited in the evening. Thus, the Tenebrae of Maundy Thursday is said on Wednesday night, the Tenebrae of Good Friday on Thursday night, etc. The structure of the Office never varies; it is essentially a form of Matins and Lauds combined.[14] It is evident that combining these two Offices created a night vigil of considerable length. Recent adaptations have tried to abbreviate it. Thus, the Office of Tenebrae provided in the *Liturgical Orders Supplementing the Service Book and Hymnal* uses primarily material from Lauds: a group of three psalms with antiphons, a brief lesson followed by the Responsory for Lent, Psalm 51, another penitential psalm, an Old Testament canticle, a *Laudate*-psalm, and the Benedictus. Each Office ends with a silent recitation of the Lord's Prayer and a collect commemorating the Passion.

The peculiar ceremony of Tenebrae, from which it derives its name, is the gradual extinguishing of lights in the church until there is total darkness. The origin of this practice is veiled in obscurity. It has been conjectured that the extinguishing of the lights was due to the coming of daylight. But in view of the fact that the proper hour for beginning Tenebrae was shortly after midnight, and that the time of the year was near the spring equinox, this explanation does not seem satisfactory. It is more likely that the candle-extinguishing ceremony was symbolic of the apparent victory of the powers of evil and the apparent failure of God's plan of salvation at our Lord's crucifixion. Today it is common, after the last candle has been extinguished, to remove the large

Christ-candle from the chancel. After a few moments of silence a loud noise is made to represent the earthquake which opened the tomb of Christ, and the Christ-candle is brought out again into the chancel. The people depart in silence.

The Tenebrae Offices might be prayed on Wednesday of Holy Week, following the Order for Public Confession; on Maundy Thursday by those keeping vigil before the reserved sacrament; and on the evening of Good Friday. (The Good Friday Liturgy is celebrated in the afternoon.) The use of Tenebrae in these ways might communicate something about the nature of the Divine Office.

The Easter Vigil. We have stressed the importance of the Easter Vigil several times in this book. An order for the Vigil is provided in the *Liturgical Orders Supplementing the Service Book and Hymnal.* Unfortunately, no music is provided in this booklet, which renders the order inadequate to the solemnity required for this "queen of all vigils." Until a fully-provisioned order is published by the ILCW, it might be desirable to use the form of the Vigil provided in the *New Roman Sacramentary.* Music for the psalms and canticles is available in a number of sources. A full musical setting of the Vigil is provided in Mason Marten's *Music for the Rites of Holy Week.* The following is a suggested order for the Vigil:

• The new fire is lighted and blessed outside the church. It is convenient to use a large barbeque grill in which to build the fire.

• The paschal candle is decorated and lighted from this fire. The assisting minister carries the paschal candle into the dark church. The other ministers and the people follow behind carrying unlighted candles. Their candles are lighted from the paschal candle at each of three stations when the assisting minister stops and sings, "The light of Christ. R/ Thanks be to God."

• The paschal candle is set in its stand next to the pulpit. The other ministers and the people go to their places.

• The assisting minister sings the Easter Proclamation (the *Exultet*) from the pulpit.

• A series of readings from the Old Testament rehearses the history of salvation. Each lesson is followed by a psalm or canticle and a collect. This is the heart of the vigil. The long series of readings characterize the vigil as a meditative service. The presiding minister should be careful to set a deliberate and leisurely pace, seeing that periods of silence are kept after each reading except the last. The number and selection of readings may vary. The traditional number was twelve. The Order of the Vigil in the SBH Supplement provides four readings; the *New Roman Sacramentary* provides seven, not including the Epistle and Gospel. The seven readings would seem to provide a good medium. But it would violate the character of the vigil if the number of readings were severely reduced and hurried through for the sake of "saving time." The people who attend should be forewarned that the vigil is a long service.

• After the last Old Testament reading, the *Gloria in excelsis* is sung. At this point the organ should be turned on and trumpets might be added. During the Gloria the Lenten colors are changed to the white or gold of Easter and the altar candles are lighted. At this time it would also be appropriate to bring the Easter lilies into the chancel.

The Prayer of the Day
The Epistle
The Alleluia
The Gospel
The Homily

• The Liturgy of Holy Baptism with Affirmation of the Baptismal Covenant. If there are no candidates for Baptism or Affirmation, there might be intercessory prayer for those coming to faith in Christ and being baptized elsewhere this night. The blessing of the font and the renewal of the baptismal covenant by the assembled congregation should take place with or without baptisms.

• The Liturgy of the Eucharistic Meal with propers for Easter. As a reminder that the vigil ended at the time of Lauds, the *Benedictus* and Psalm 150 replace the *Nunc dimittis* after the Communion.

• After the Benediction, the assisting minister exclaims: "Christ is risen." The people respond: "He is risen indeed. Alleluia."

Easter. In the new calendar Easter is not a one-day celebration but a fifty-day celebration. During this time, said St. John Chrysostom, "we have unending holiday." This week of weeks of celebration, culminating on the Day of Pentecost, should enable us to rediscover the ingredients of true festivity. The sense of new life, renewal, restoration, transformation, rebirth, etc., which is engendered by the message of Easter can only erupt in celebration and affirmation; and those are the principal elements of a festival.[15] The message of Christ's resurrection and glorification should be buttressed by all the liturgical elements throughout this fifty-day season, including the hymns and anthems.

The Sixth Sunday of Easter maintains the tradition of the former *Cantate* Sunday. The psalms appointed for this day suggest that the contribution of new church music be recognized on this day: "Sing to the Lord a new song." It's a day on which the choir might work up some special anthems and on which the congregation might be exposed to some new hymns.

Ascension. A special custom on The Ascension of our Lord is the snuffing out of the paschal candle during the Gospel reading. CW-6, p. 88, suggests that "The candle may then be moved near the baptismal font and lighted at baptisms throughout the year to emphasize their resurrection character." If the paschal candle is not extinguished at the service on Ascension Day it should be kept burning until the Day of Pentecost.

Pentecost. The traditional hymn for this day is *Veni Creator Spiritus* (SBH # 117 and # 124; LH # 233 and # 236). Seven votive lights might be placed on the altar to symbolize the seven-fold gifts of the Holy Spirit. Like Easter, Pentecost is an appropriate day for Holy Baptism and Affirmation of the Baptismal Covenant. To dramatize the "Pentecostal explosion," the whole congregation might process out of the building during the closing hymn. This would underscore the idea of dismissal to mission. After the Day of Pentecost the time of holiday is ended; the time for doing the work of the kingdom has begun. The festival half-year of the church is ended; the time for the steady building up of the church has begun.

The Sundays after Pentecost should be characterized by a kind of liturgical sameness. The liturgy should be varied only by the contents of the propers. Patterns of corporate behavior and belief can be established only by unvarying repetition. This repetition of patterns fosters community cohesion and identity. Moreover, the festival seasons of the church year are then highlighted by the fact that their liturgies do depart from the usual way of doing things.

There are some festivals and commemorations which occur during the long Pentecost season. The Festival of the Holy Trinity affords an occasion to recite the Athanasian Creed since it is a fuller profession of the mystery of the Godhead than the Nicene or Apostles' Creeds. The Festival of the Holy Cross on September 14, or the Sunday nearest it, provides an opportunity for a parish rally day after the scattering effect of summer vacation. Reformation Day gives Lutherans an opportunity to celebrate their heritage by using liturgical and hymnic material from the Reformation period. All Saints' Day provides an occasion for remembering the faithful departed of the parish in the general intercessions.

Some of the *customs and ceremonies* we have mentioned, especially during the festival half-year of the calendar, help to establish the relationship between what has been called "liturgy and life." In fact, there is no dichotomy between liturgy and life because liturgy is the public work of the people of God. If there is no correlation between liturgy and life, one or the other is a pretense. This relationship can be reinforced through the use of such customs and ceremonies as advent wreathes, crismon trees, and baptismal candles which can be used in family homes as well as in the church building. Devotional offices surrounding the lighting of the Advent wreath, the Christmas tree, or the baptismal candle help build a bridge between the gathered and the scattered community. These little customs bring the sacramental economy of salvation right into earthly homes. They are as close as Lutherans get to what are called "popular devotions" in the Roman Catholic Church. Fr. Carl Dehne defines devotions as "popular" that (1) "are pitched at and practiced by ordinary Christians," (2) appeal to a relatively large number of people, and (3) "are capable of communal celebration and are typically so celebrated." [16]

The appeal of these devotions in family celebrations is growing. The practice of them undoubtedly results in edification, but their primary value is that they facilitate devotional expression. They are ceremonialized, and this helps average Christians express themselves in prayer in ways which they might otherwise not be capable of doing. The fact that these customs and ceremonies partake of archaic qualities is also to the good. As the anthropologist, Victor Turner, has written, "It is a mistake to think that the archaic is the fossilized or surpassed. The archaic can be as contemporary as nuclear physics." [17] Liturgical customs and forms are not "dead" if they are used creatively and freely as means of devotional expression and celebration. These customs and ceremonies appeal to people because it is true of contemporary people as of archaic people that they have a need to express creature-feelings of awe, overpoweringness and fascination before the *mysterium tremendum*.[18] We are learning once again that meaningful worship requires a sense of transcendence.

Epilog:

Why All this Emphasis on Ritual?

It cannot be emphasized too strongly that the whole thrust of liturgical renewal has been the renewal of the church as the body of Christ. The New Testament description of this body suggests that all the members of it should be involved in the life and mission of the church. There is no doubt that many church members would rather remain spectators than become participants. So liturgical renewal does not interest them. They don't want to be bothered or impinged upon when they come to church. They want to be left alone. If New Testament theology cannot convince such people of the "rightness" of what is happening, they must be commended to pastoral care.

Those who are actively committed to the life and mission of the church will understand that *total involvement* means just that: the use of the whole body in worship with all its senses, limbs, and faculties. The body is the temple of the Holy Spirit. This is the Spirit of the risen Christ who comes to dwell in us and expel the *rigor mortis* from our bodies so that we can be up and about, praising God and being together with God's people, living the life of faith nurtured by Word and Sacrament and caring for one another in the hard-nosed realities of this world.[19]

The emphasis on ritual action serves to combat passive faith and to get people engaged with one another in common work.

If the members of the body of Christ cannot be together un-afraid of each other's touch, it is unlikely that they will be able to become involved with the "great unwashed" of this world who are not yet members of the household of faith. It just may be that in the actions of the liturgy we will find new patterns of Christian living which will have far greater social and inter-personal effectiveness in the generations ahead than the purely inward religion of the generations immediately passed. Such, at any rate, is our pious *desideratum* and our fervent prayer.

Notes

Chapter One

1. See Carl Volz, "Lex Orandi, Lex Credendi; or Prayer and Profession," *Response* XIV, No. 2 (1974), 17-22.

2. Susanne Langer, *Philosophy in a New Key* (New York: Penguin Books, 1948), pp. 237-38.

3. See Mircea Eliade, *Cosmos and History. The Myth of the Eternal Return* (New York: Harper Torchbooks, 1959).

4. Aidan Kavanagh, "The Role of Ritual in Personal Development," in *The Roots of Ritual,* ed. James Shaughnessy (Grand Rapids: Eerdmans 1973), pp. 148-49.

5. *Luther's Works,* American Edition, Vol. 22 (St. Louis: Concordia, 1957), p. 105.

6. AC 14; Ap. 13:7-9. See Arthur Carl Piepkorn, "The Sacred Ministry and Holy Ordination in the Symbolical Books of the Lutheran Church," in *Lutherans and Catholics in Dialogue IV: Eucharist and Ministry* (U.S.A. National Committee of the Lutheran World Federation and the Bishops' Committee for Ecumenical and Interreligious Affairs, 1970), 101-19.

7. Thus John H. Elliott, *The Elect and the Holy. Supplements to Novum Testamentum* XII (Leiden: Brill, 1966). See also Raymond Brown, *Priest and Bishop: Biblical Reflections* (New York: Paulist, 1970).

8. Ap 7:28; *The Book of Concord,* ed. and trans. Theodore G. Tappert (Philadelphia: Fortress, 1959), p. 173.

9. *Ibid.,* 13:11-12; p. 212.

10. See my article, "Church Structure: Our's or the Spirit's?" *Dialog* 12 (Winter 1973), 66-69. (Some lines are unfortunately marred by shoddy typesetting.)

11. Robert Hovda, "Training, Recognition for Official Ministries besides the Clergy's," *Living Worship* 9, No. 5 (May 1973).

Chapter Two

1. W. Jardine Grisbrooke, "A Contemporary Liturgical Problem: The Divine Office and Public Worship," *Studia Liturgica* 8, No. 3 (1971/72), 130.

2. *Ibid.*

3. *Ibid.*

4. Alexander Schmemann, *Introduction to Liturgical Theology* (Portland: The American Orthodox Press, 1966), p. 88.

5. *Ibid.*, p. 102.

6. *Ibid.*, p. 107.

7. *Ibid.*, p. 108.

8. See Pierre Salmon, *The Breviary Through the Centuries*, trans. Sister David Mary (Collegeville: The Liturgical Press, 1962), pp. 1-41.

9. See Martin Luther, "Concerning the Order of Public Worship," 1523, *Luther's Works*, Vol. 53 (Philadelphia: Fortress, 1965), 11-14; E. C. Ratcliff, "The Choir Offices," in *Liturgy and Worship*, ed. W. K. Lowther Clark (London: SPCK, 1932), esp. pp. 267-68.

10. See Josef Jungmann, *The Early Liturgy to the Time of Gregory the Great* (Notre Dame: University of Notre Dame Press, 1958), pp. 97-108; 278-287.

11. See Juan Mateos, "The Origins of the Divine Office," *Worship* 41 (1967), 477-485 and "The Morning and Evening Office," *Worship* 42 (1968), 31-47. Mateos has studied the survival of the Cathedral Office among the Chaldeans. A similar survival can be seen at the other extreme of Christendom, in the Mozarabic Office of the Cathedral at Toledo.

12. William G. Storey, "The Liturgy of the Hours: Cathedral Versus Monastery," *Worship* 50 (1976), 55-57.

13. It is evident that St. Augustine frequently preached at Vespers; see F. Van der Meer, *Augustine the Bishop*, trans. B. Battershaw and G. R. Lamb (New York: Sheed and Ward, 1961), pp. 172, 345. Neither the *Apostolic Constitutions* nor Egeria in her *Journal*, however, make any mention of preaching at morning and evening prayer although they comment on it at the Eucharist.

14. Storey, 58.

15. Grisbrooke, *Studia Liturgica* 9/1 (1973), 3-4.

16. *Ibid.*, 7-8.

17. Louis Bouyer, *Liturgical Piety* (Notre Dame: University of Notre Dame Press, 1954), p. 194.

18. Alexander Schmemann, *For the Life of the World* (New

York: National Student Christian Federation, 1963; reprint St. Vladimir Press, 1974), p. 42.

19. Grisbrooke, 12.

20. W. S. Porter, "Early Spanish Monasticism," *Laudate* (Quarterly Review of Nashdom Abbey) 10 (1932); 11 (1933); 12 (1934).

21. *Morning Praise and Evensong,* ed. William G. Storey, Frank Quinn, O. P. and David Wright O. P. (Notre Dame: Fides, 1973).

Chapter Three

1. Tappert, pp. 348-49.

2. Edmund Schlink, *The Doctrine of Baptism,* trans. Herbert J. A. Bouman (St. Louis: Concordia, 1972), p. 58.

3. Tappert, p. 178.

4. The notion must be avoided that the children of Christian parents are "holy and children of God even without or before Baptism," *Formula of Concord,* Epitome XII, 8; Tappert, p. 498.

5. Mircea Eliade, *Rites and Symbols of Initiation* (New York: Harper Torchbook, 1958), p. x.

6. Tappert, p. 349.

7. Schlink, pp. 77-78.

8. For fuller treatment of the provisional Liturgy of Holy Baptism see my articles: "The Shape and Content of Christian Initiation: An Exposition of the new Lutheran Liturgy of Holy Baptism," *Dialog* 14 (Spring 1975), 97-107; "A New Baptismal Rite: Toward Revitalizing the Whole Community," *Currents in Theology and Mission* 2 (Concordia Seminary in Exile: August 1975), 206-214.

9. Eugene L. Brand, "New Accents in Baptism and the Eucharist," in *Worship: Good News in Action,* ed. Mandus Egge (Minneapolis: Augsburg, 1973), p. 71.

10. Aidan Kavanagh, "Christian Initiation of Adults: The Rites," *Worship* 48 (1974), 325.

11. E. C. Whitaker, *Documents of the Baptismal Liturgy* (London: SPCK, 1970), p. 132.

12. Joseph Sittler *Essays on Nature and Grace* (Philadelphia: Fortress, 1972), pp. 93-94.

13. See my article, "An End for Confirmation?" *Currents in Theology and Mission* 3 (February 1976), 45-52.

Chapter Four

1. Schmemann, *Introduction to Liturgical Theology*, p. 133.

2. See John P. Dolan, *History of the Reformation* (New York: Mentor-Omega, 1965), pp. 196 ff.

3. See Oliver K. Olson, "Litury as 'Action,'" *Dialog* 14 (Spring 1975), 108-113.

4. Robert Jenson, "Worship as Drama," in *The Futurist Option*, with Carl E. Braaten (New York: Newman, 1970), pp. 159-60.

5. *Ibid.*, p. 182.

6. James F. White, *New Forms of Worship* (Nashville: Abingdon, 1971), p. 43.

7. E. A. Sovik, *Architecture for Worship* (Minneapolis: Augsburg, 1973), p. 19. See also Ralph Van Loon, *Space for Worship* (Board of Publication of the Lutheran Church in America, 1975).

8. For additional ideas on decorating the worship space see James Notebaart, "Shaping the Environment of Celebration: Art, Design for Visual Order and Beauty," *Living Worship* 10, No. 3 (March 1974).

Chapter Five

1. Schmemann, *For the Life of the World*, p. 69.

2. Eugene L. Brand, *The Rite Thing* (Minneapolis: Augsburg, 1970), p. 37.

3. The concept of "the worship team" is developed by Ralph Van Loon in *Planning Parish Worship* (Philadelphia: Parish Life Press, 1976). Pastor Van Loon built this concept into the outline for the course on "The Pastor as Worship Leader and Coordinator" which I wrote for the 1975 Lutheran Institutes on Worship and Music. Our suggestions are conveniently parallel.

4. See Edward F. Peters, "Luther and the Principle: Outside of the Use There Is No Sacrament," *Concordia Theological Monthly* 42 (November 1971), 643-52.

Chapter Six

1. Frederick A. Rowe, *I Launch at Paradise. A Consideration of John Donne, Poet and Preacher* (London: Epworth 1964), p. 196.

2. Ernest Koenker, *The Liturgical Renaissance in the Roman*

Catholic Church (St. Louis: Concordia, 1954) describes the patristic ideals of the liturgical movement in chapter IV.

3. See Bouyer, *Liturgical Piety,* chapter VI, pp. 70ff.

4. *Luther's Works,* Vol. 53, p. 90.

5. See Friedrich Blume, *Protestant Church Music,* Eng. trans. (New York: Norton, 1974), pp. 1ff., 125ff., 405ff.

6. For a useful survey of the evolution of the Liturgy see Theodore Klauser, *A Short History of the Western Liturgy,* trans. John Halliburton (New York: Oxford University Press, 1969).

7. See C. W. Dugmore, *The Influence of the Synagogue Upon the Divine Office* (Westminster: Faith, 1964), pp. 71ff.

8. Gregory Dix, *The Shape of the Liturgy* (London: Dacre, 1945), pp. 48ff.

9. Oliver K. Olson, "Contemporary Trends in Liturgy Viewed from the Perspective of Classical Lutheran Theoloy," *Lutheran Quarterly* 26 (1974), 125 ff. See my reply: "Contemporary Liturgical Theology," *Response* 14 (1974), 10-17.

10. *Formula of Concord,* Solid Declaration VII, 83-84; Tappert, p. 584.

11. See Josef A. Jungmann, *The Early Liturgy to the Time of Gregory the Great* (University of Notre Dame Press, 1959), pp. 253ff.

12. *Luther's Works,* Vol. 53, pp. 28-29.

13. Anton Baumstark, *Comparative Liturgy,* Eng. trans. (Westminster: Newman, 1958), p. 27.

14. See John W. Tyrer, *Historical Survey of Holy Week: Its Services and Ceremonies,* Alcuin Club Collection No. XXIX (London, 1932), pp. 81-84.

15. See Josef Pieper, *In Tune with the World. A Theory of Festivity* (Chicago: Franciscan Herald Press, 1973), pp. 25ff.

16. Carl Dehne, "Roman Catholic Popular Devotions," *Worship* 49 (1975), 449.

17. Victor Turner, "Passages, Margins, and Poverty: Religious Symbols of Communitas," *Worship* 46 (1972), 391.

18. See the classic study of Rudolf Otto, *The Idea of the Holy,* trans. John W. Harvey (New York: Oxford, 1955).

19. See the chapter on the "Spirituality of Hope" in Carl E. Braaten, *Christ and Counter-Christ. Apocalyptic Themes in Theology and Culture* (Philadelphia: Fortress 1972), pp. 82-100.

Bibliography

I: For Worship Planning

The following books ought to be included in the parish library as basic resources of liturgical material for the use of pastors, musicians, and worship and music committees in worship planning.

A. Episcopal

Authorized Services 1973. New York: Church Hymnal Corporation, 1973.

The Hymnal 1940. New York: The Church Pension Fund, 1940.

The Book of Common Prayer (USA). New York: The Church Pension Fund, 1945.

The Book of Offices. Services for certain occasions not provided in the Book of Common Prayer. New York: The Church Pension Fund, 1960.

The Standing Liturgical Commission of the Episcopal Church: Provisional liturgical material published in the *Prayer Book Studies* (PBS) series.

Services for Trial Use. Includes forms of the Eucharistic Liturgy with Collects and the Lectionary of the Church Year from PBS 19.

The Daily Office Revised. The revised lectionary for Sundays, Fixed Holy Days, and the Office Lectionary for Weekends and moveable Holy Days, together with Tables of Psalms. PBS 25.

Lesser Feasts and Fasts. A revised edition of the Propers for Weekdays in Lent and for Black Letter Days, together with biographical sketches and historical notes regarding the days of optional observance.

Prayers, Thanksgivings, and Litanies. A collection of prayers in traditional and contemporary styles suitable for use with the Daily Office and with the Holy Eucharist. PBS 25.

Holy Baptism together with a Form of Confirmation or the Laying-On of Hands by the Bishop with the Affimation of Baptismal Vows. PBS 26.

All *Prayer Book Studies* are published by the Church Hymnal Corporation.

B. Lutheran

(1) The Lutheran Church—Missouri Synod
The Lutheran Agenda. St. Louis: Concordia, 1936.
The Lutheran Hymnal. St. Louis: Concordia, 1941.
Proposed Rites for Holy Baptism, The Ordination of a Minister, and the Burial of the Dead. St. Louis: Concordia, n. d.
Worship Supplement. St. Louis: Concordia, 1969.

(2) Lutheran Church in America and The American Lutheran Church
The Service Book and Hymnal of the Lutheran Church in America. Philadelphia: The Board of Publication of the Lutheran Church in America, 1958; Minneapolis: Augsburg, 1958.
The Occasional Services. Minneapolis: Augsburg, 1962.
Holy Week and Easter: Liturgical Orders Supplementing the Service Book and Hymnal. Philadelphia: Fortress, 1968.
The Psalmody of the Day for Series A, B, and C and Lesser Festivals. Philadelphia: Fortress, n. d.

(3) The Inter-Lutheran Commission on Worship: Provisional liturgical material published in the *Contemporary Worship* (CW) series.
CW-1: 21 Contemporary Hymns
CW-2: The Holy Communion in four musical settings
CW-3: The Marriage Service in Two Forms
CW-4: Hymns for Baptism and Holy Communion
CW-5: Services of the Word for Advent, Christmas, Lent, Easter, and Two for General Use
CW-6: The Church Year Calendar and Lectionary
CW-7: The Liturgy of Holy Baptism
CW-8: Affirmation of the Baptismal Covenant
CW-9: Daily Prayer of the Church
CW-10: Burial of the Dead

C. Roman Catholic

The Roman Missal: Lectionary for the Mass. Collegeville: Liturgical Press, 1970.

The Roman Missal: Sacramentary for the Mass. Collegeville: Liturgical Press, 1974.

English Ritual (Collectio Rituum). Collegeville: Liturgical Press, 1964.

D. Additional Hymnals and Psalmbooks

Book of Worship for U.S. Forces. Washington, D.C.: The U.S. Government Printing Office, 1974.

The English Hymnal. London: Oxford University Press, 1933.

The Grail Gelineau Psalter. 150 Psalms and 18 Canticles. Chicago: G.I.A. Publications, 1972.

Hymns Ancient and Modern. London: William Clowes and Sons, 1922.

Hymnal for Young Christians. Chicago and Los Angeles: F.E.L. Church Publications, 1968. Published in congregational and accompaniment editions: Ecumenical Version and Roman Catholic Mass Supplement Version.

Martens, Mason. *Music for the Holy Eucharist and the Daily Office.* New York: The Church Army in the U.S.A., 1971. Contains simple chant settings for the Liturgy, a selection of psalms and canticles for the Office.

Psalms for the Church Year for Congregation and Choir. Minneapolis: Augsburg, 1975. Published in congregational and choir —accompaniment editions.

E. The Divine Office

Storey, William G., ed. *Morning Praise and Evensong.* Notre Dame: Fides, 1973. One typical morning and evening office is published in a pamphlet for congregational use.

_____., *Praise Him! A Prayer Book for Today's Christian.* Notre Dame: Ave Maria, 1973.

_____., *Bless the Lord! A Prayer Book for Advent, Christmas, Lent and Eastertide.* Notre Dame: Ave Maria, 1974.

The Taize Office. Trans. by Anthony Brown. London: Faith, 1966.

F. Holy Week and Easter

Jasper, C. D., ed. *Holy Week Services.* By the Joint Liturgical Group. London: SPCK and Epworth, 1971.

Jones, C. P. M., ed. *A Manual for Holy Week*. London: SPCK, 1967. 20 authors. Includes select bibliography, pp. 203-206.

The Liturgy of Holy Week. Arranged for use in parishes. Collegeville: Liturgical Press, 1965.

Martens, Mason. *Music for the Rites of Holy Week*. New York: The Church Army in the U.S.A., 1972.

Shepherd, Massey H. *Holy Week Offices*. Services Supplementary to the American Prayer Book. Seabury, 1958.

G. Manuals

Many of ceremonial directions in the following works have been rendered obsolete by contemporary styles of celebration. But there is still much in these classics which is useful. Everything in them is adaptable to new situations, so they should also be included in parish libraries as resources for worship planning.

A Directory of Ceremonial, 2 Volumes. London: Oxford University Press, 1931.

Fortescue, Adrian and O'Connell, J. B. *The Ceremonies of the Roman Rite Described*. Twelfth revised ed. London: Burns and Oates, 1962.

Lang, Paul H. D. *Ceremony and Celebration*. St. Louis: Concordia, 1965.

Reed, Luther D. *Worship*. Philadelphia: Muhlenberg, 1959.

Schmitz, Walter J. *Sanctuary Manual*. Milwaukee. Bruce, 1965.

Weiser, Francis X. *Handbook of Christian Feasts and Customs: The Year of the Lord in Liturgy and Folklore*. New York: Harcourt, Brace, 1952.

H. For Study

The following works provide useful historical information which might be needed in worship planning.

Davies, J. G., ed. *A Dictionary of Christian Worship*. New York: Macmillan, 1972. Contains 361 articles written by 65 different liturgical experts representing the most up-to-date research on each topic.

Dix, Gregory. *The Shape of the Liturgy*. London: Dacre, 1945; repr. 1960.

Jungmann, Josef A. *The Early Liturgy to the Time of Gregory the Great*. Notre Dame: The University of Notre Dame Press, 1959.

Reed, Luther D. *The Lutheran Liturgy*. Philadelphia: Fortress, 1959.

Routley, Eric. *Hymns and the Faith*. Seabury, 1956.

Ryden, E. E. *The Story of Christian Hymnody*. Rock Island: Augustana, 1959.

Thurston, Herbert and Attwater, Donald, editors. *Butler's Lives of the Saints*. Four volumes. Palm Publishers, 1956.

I. Liturgical Periodicals

The only way to keep a working library current is through subscription to several periodicals. The following would help keep worship planning current.

Accent on Worship, Music and the Arts. Published five times a year for the Members of the Lutheran Society for Worship, Music and the Arts.

Church Music. Published semiannually by Concordia.

Church Music Memo. Published three times a year under the auspices of the Division for Life and Mission of the American Lutheran Church, the Division for Parish Services of the Lutheran Church in America, and the Commission on Worship of the Lutheran Church—Missouri Synod.

Christian Celebration. Published four times a year from 10-12 High Street, Great Wakering, SS3 OEQ, England.

Hucusque. Published by the Murphy Center for Liturgical Research, Box 81, University of Notre Dame, Notre Dame, Indiana 46556.

Journal of Church Music. Published monthly by Fortress.

Living Worship. Published monthly by the Liturgical Conference, 1330 Massachusetts Avenue, N.W., Washington, D.C. 20005.

Liturgy. Journal of the Liturgical Conference. Membership fee is $15 a year, which includes a subscription to the journal.

Response. Journal of the Lutheran Society for Worship, Music and the Arts. Membership fee is $10 regular, $15 sustaining, which includes a subscription to the Journal. The Journal may be subscripted to separately for $5 per year.

Studia Liturgica. An international ecumenical quarterly for liturgical research and renewal. Published by the Liturgical Ecumenical Center Trust, Box 25088, Rotterdam, Holland.

Worship. Published at Collegeville, Minnesota, by the Benedictines of St. John's Abbey.

II: Popular Works in Liturgical Renewal

From the multitude of books dealing with liturgical renewal in recent years, the following ten are recommended to pastors and worship leaders to help them "bone up" on the theories which have accompanied liturgical renewal.

Brand, Eugene L. *The Rite Thing* (Minneapolis: Augsburg 1970). An exploration of a number of prominent accents in contemporary liturgical theology and practice: involvement in the action of liturgy; worship as the coordinated effort of the many members of the one body in Christ; the concept of commemoration in sacramental theology; the sacrificial aspect of worship and the restoration of the offertory; and the eschatological dimension of Christian worship.

Brand, Eugene L. *Baptism: A Pastoral Perspective* (Minneapolis: Augsburg, 1975). Important elements of theology and practice which lie behind the reform of the baptismal rite and the renewal of Christian initiation are pulled together. While the book is not written as an apologetic for the ILCW provisional liturgy of Holy Baptism (CW-7), it is good background reading for that rite.

Egge, Mandus, ed. *Worship: Good News in Action* (Minneapolis: Augsburg, 1973). This is a collection of the major addresses delivered at the 1973 Inter-Lutheran Conference on Worship held in Minneapolis by Joseph Sittler, Henry E. Horn, James F. White, Jaroslav Pelikan, Eugene L. Brand, Edward A. Sovik, Daniel B. Stevick, and Wayne E. Saffen.

Horn, Henry E. *Worship in Crisis* (Philadelphia: Fortress, 1972). An analysis of why a crisis in worship emerged from the upheavals of the 1960s combined with a critique of the developing new forms and styles of worship with suggestions as to "where we must go from here."

Koenker, Ernest B. *The Liturgical Renaissance in the Roman Catholic Church* (St. Louis: Concordia, 1954; reprint 1966). A scholarly analysis of the theological theories and pastoral work of the liturgical movement and how it succeeded in reforming liturgical life in the Roman Catholic Church. Koenker, a Lutheran, shows how this "liturgical renaissance" in many ways fulfilled and moved beyond the goals of the sixteenth century Reformation. It is perhaps the most thorough and systematic study of the liturgical movement available.

Lindemann, Herbert F. *The New Mood in Lutheran Worship* (Minneapolis: Augsburg, 1971). Pastor Lindemann traces the progress of the liturgical movement in the Lutheran Church since the beginning of this century. His conversational style brings the goals of liturgical renewal down to clear, practical concepts, but not without creating a feeling of tension between the actual and the ideal.

Micks, Marianne H. *The Future Present. The Phenomenon of Christian Worship* (New York: Seabury, 1970). Working from an informed knowledge of contemporary philosophy and theology, Dr. Micks presents worship as a complex response of human beings to the experience of space and time, taste and touch, sound and silence. She probes the role of play, dance, and the total use of the body in the action of worship.

Murphy Center for Liturgical Research, *Made, Not Born. New Perspectives on Christian Initiation and the Catechumenate* (Notre Dame: University of Notre Dame Press, 1976). The papers edited in this book deal with the historical, theological, and pastoral aspects of Christian initiation. They open up new possibilities for the role of the catechumenate in the making of Christians. Contributors are Aidan Kavanagh, Reginald Fuller, Robert M. Grant, Nathan Mitchell, Leonel L. Mitchell, Daniel Stevick, Robert Hovda, and Ralph Keifer.

Shaughnessy, James, ed. *The Roots of Ritual* (Grand Rapids: Eerdmans, 1973). This is the first book published by the Murphy Center for Liturgical Research at the University of Notre Dame. The essays collected in this book show how persons working in different fields view ritual as a basic human language. The contributors are Robert Bellah, sociologist; David Burrell, philosophic theologian; Jon Christopher Crocker, sociologist; Edward Fischer, communicator; Aidan Kavanagh, liturgiologist; Margaret Mead, anthropologist; Patrick Quinn, architect; Jonathon Smith, historian of religions; and Brian Wicker, literary critic. They all show, in their various ways, that modern man has not outgrown his need for ritual, but rather that it is a basic and essential form of communication.

Sovik, Edward A. *Architecture for Worship* (Minneapolis: Augsburg, 1973). A radical critique of traditional church architecture with a plea for architecture which is more flexible, functional, and expressive of the Gospel. Sovik argues for the use of the centrum plan and suggests ways of renewing old church buildings.